perfect
chinese

This is a Parragon Publishing book
First published in 2007

Parragon Publishing
Queen Street House
4 Queen Street
Bath BA1 1HE, UK

Copyright © Parragon Books Ltd 2007
Designed by Terry Jeavons & Company

ISBN 978-1-4054-9181-5

Printed in China

This book uses imperial, metric, and US cup measurements. Follow the same units of measurement throughout; do not mix imperial and metric. All spoon measurements are level, unless otherwise stated: teaspoons are assumed to be 5ml, and tablespoons are assumed to be 15ml. Unless otherwise stated, milk is assumed to be whole, eggs and individual fruits such as bananas are medium, and pepper is freshly ground black pepper.

Recipes using raw or very lightly cooked eggs should be avoided by infants, the elderly, pregnant women, convalescents, and anyone suffering from an illness. Pregnant and breast-feeding women are advised to avoid eating peanuts and peanut products.

perfect
chinese

introduction	4
soups & appetizers	6
main dishes	52
noodles & rice	116
vegetables & side dishes	172
desserts	218
index	240

introduction

Most people enjoy good Chinese food, and this is perhaps because the Chinese people's respect for their cuisine is reflected in the food itself. Cooking is considered to be an art, not a necessary chore, and indeed Chinese dishes are every bit as beautiful to look at as they are delicious to eat.

A vast population inhabiting an often rugged, agriculturally barren landscape has led to creative use of the available ingredients. Many crops, including potatoes, tomatoes, and eggplants, were introduced by foreigners and have been absorbed into the Chinese culinary culture mainly because they grow successfully in poor soil.

Traditionally in China, and still today, there is a vitally important relationship between food and health, This manifests in two distinct ways. Firstly, there is a closely observed balance between carbohydrate foods,

mostly in the form of rice or grains, and all other foods, from meat, fish, and seafood to fresh and preserved vegetables. Secondly, foods are further divided into two groups, *yin* and *yang*. Yang are "heating" foods, such as beef, carrots, and chiles, associated with masculinity, while yin are "cooling" foods—crab, watercress, and cucumber—associated with femininity. Thus, the composition of a meal takes account not only of what is in season or looks good at the market, but also of the age, gender, and state of health of the diners, and the weather!

If all you want, however, is an appetizing meal with marvelous color, flavor, and texture, quick and easy to cook, simply choose your favorite recipes and enjoy yourself! To eat Chinese-style,

especially when you have guests, serve several dishes and have a little of everything—remember to aim for balance. Pretty Chinese serving bowls will enhance the menu, and of course chopsticks add to the fun.

A toast to your very good health!

soups &
appetizers

Soups are one of the mainstays of the Chinese diet. They are almost exclusively light, clear broths with the addition of a little meat, seafood, or bean curd, and sometimes noodles, together with seasonal vegetables and fresh herbs. They are not served, Western-style, at the start of a meal, but are eaten throughout the meal, or even at the end—delicate Szechuan Pumpkin Soup, for example, freshens the palate after a series of spicy dishes. Soups are also eaten for breakfast, or as a snack throughout the day, and are certainly nutritious and satisfying enough to make a perfect light lunch or supper dish. Wonton Soup is definitely a meal in itself—use good quality chicken stock as the base and be generous with the wontons.

The Chinese do not necessarily serve separate Western-style "appetizers" either, but have a vast array of snack foods in their culinary repertoire, to be found on food stalls everywhere—the things we all know and love, such as Spring Rolls, Shrimp Toasts, Soy Chicken Wings, and Crispy Crab Wontons. These make excellent appetizers in a marriage of Western and Eastern cuisines, and you can add a few dishes that you might not have tried—soft, melting Onion Pancakes, Tea-scented Eggs, and Lettuce Wraps, which your guests can assemble themselves.

wonton soup

ingredients

SERVES 6

30 square wonton skins

1 egg white, lightly beaten

2 tbsp finely chopped
scallion, to serve

1 tbsp chopped cilantro
leaves, to garnish

filling

6 oz/175 g ground pork,
not too lean

8 oz/225 g raw shrimp,
shelled, deveined, and
chopped

$1/2$ tsp finely chopped fresh
gingerroot

1 tbsp light soy sauce

1 tbsp Shaoxing rice wine

2 tsp finely chopped scallion

pinch of sugar

pinch of white pepper

dash of sesame oil

soup

64 fl oz/2 liters/8 cups
chicken stock

2 tsp salt

$1/2$ tsp white pepper

method

1 Mix together the filling ingredients and stir well until the texture is thick and pasty. Set aside for at least 20 minutes.

2 To make the wontons, place a teaspoon of the filling in the center of a skin. Brush the edges with a little egg white. Bring the opposite points toward each other and press the edges together, creating a flower-like shape. Repeat with the remaining skins and filling.

3 To make the soup, bring the stock to a boil and add the salt and pepper. Boil the wontons in the stock for about 5 minutes, or until the skins begin to wrinkle around the filling.

4 To serve, put the scallion in individual bowls, then spoon in the wontons and soup and top with the cilantro.

crab & corn soup

ingredients

SERVES 4

4 oz/115 g fresh or frozen
   crabmeat

20 fl oz/625 ml/2$^1\!/_2$ cups
   water

15 oz/425 g canned
   cream-style corn, drained

$^1\!/_2$ tsp salt

pinch of pepper

2 tsp cornstarch, dissolved in
   2 tbsp water (optional)

1 egg, beaten

method

1 If using frozen crabmeat, blanch the flesh in boiling water for 30 seconds. Remove with a slotted spoon and set aside.

2 In a large pan, bring the water to a boil with the crab and corn and let simmer for 2 minutes. Season with the salt and pepper. Stir in the cornstarch, if using, and continue stirring until the soup has thickened. Rapidly stir in the egg and serve.

ground beef & cilantro soup

ingredients

SERVES 4–6

8 oz/225 g/2 cups
    ground beef
48 fl oz/1.6 liters/6$^{1}/_{4}$ cups
    chicken stock
3 egg whites, lightly beaten
1 tsp salt
$^{1}/_{2}$ tsp white pepper
1 tbsp finely chopped fresh
    gingerroot
1 tbsp finely chopped scallion
4–5 tbsp finely chopped
    cilantro, tough stems
    discarded

marinade

1 tsp salt
1 tsp sugar
1 tsp Shaoxing rice wine
1 tsp light soy sauce

method

1 Combine all the ingredients for the marinade in a bowl and marinate the beef for 20 minutes.

2 Bring the stock to a boil. Add the beef, stirring to break up any clumps, and let simmer for 10 minutes.

3 Slowly add the egg whites, stirring rapidly so that they form into fine shreds. Add the salt and pepper and taste to check the seasoning.

4 To serve, place the gingerroot, scallion, and cilantro in the base of individual bowls and pour the soup on top.

bean curd & bean sprout soup

ingredients

SERVES 4–6

10 oz/280 g spareribs, cut
　　into small pieces
40 fl oz/1.25 liters/5 cups
　　water
2 tomatoes, seeded and
　　coarsely chopped
3 thin slices fresh gingerroot
5 oz/140 g/scant 1 cup
　　bean sprouts
2 tsp salt
7 oz/200 g soft bean curd,
　　cut into 1-inch/2.5-cm
　　cubes

method

1 Bring a pan of water to a boil and blanch the spareribs for about 30 seconds. Skim the water, then remove the ribs and set aside.

2 Bring the measured water to a boil and add the spareribs, tomatoes, and gingerroot. After 10 minutes, remove the tomato skins from the water. Add the bean sprouts and salt, then cover and let simmer for 1 hour. Add the bean curd cubes and let simmer for an additional 2 minutes, then serve.

hot-&-sour soup

ingredients

SERVES 4–5

3 dried Chinese mushrooms,
    soaked in warm water for
    20 minutes
4 oz/115 g pork loin
2 oz/55 g/$\frac{1}{2}$ cup fresh or
    canned bamboo shoots,
    rinsed (if using fresh
    shoots, boil in water first
    for 30 minutes)
8 oz/225 g firm bean curd
30 fl oz/940 ml/3$\frac{3}{4}$ cups
    chicken stock
1 tbsp Shaoxing rice wine
1 tbsp light soy sauce
1$\frac{1}{2}$ tbsp white rice vinegar
1 tsp salt
1 tsp white pepper
1 egg, lightly beaten

method

1 Squeeze out any excess water from the mushrooms, then finely slice, discarding any tough stems. Finely slice the pork, bamboo shoots, and bean curd, all to a similar size.

2 Bring the stock to a boil. Add the pork and boil over high heat for 2 minutes. Add the mushrooms and bamboo shoots and boil for an additional 2 minutes. Next, add the Shaoxing, light soy sauce, rice vinegar, salt, and pepper. Bring back to a boil and let simmer, covered, for 5 minutes. Add the bean curd and boil, uncovered, for 2 minutes.

3 To serve, rapidly stir in the egg until it has formed fine shreds. Serve immediately.

whole chicken soup

ingredients

SERVES 6–8

$3^1/_2$ oz/100 g Yunnan ham or
   ordinary ham, chopped

2 dried Chinese mushrooms,
   soaked in warm water for
   20 minutes

3 oz/85 g/$^3/_4$ cup fresh or
   canned bamboo shoots,
   rinsed (if using fresh
   shoots, boil in water first
   for 30 minutes)

1 whole chicken

1 tbsp slivered scallion

8 slices fresh gingerroot

8 oz/225 g lean pork,
   chopped

2 tsp Shaoxing rice wine

96 fl oz/3 liters/12 cups water

2 tsp salt

$10^1/_2$ oz/300 g Chinese
   cabbage, cut into large
   chunks

sesame & scallion dipping sauce

2 tbsp light soy sauce

$^1/_4$ tsp sesame oil

2 tsp finely chopped scallion

method

1 To make the dipping sauce, combine the ingredients and set aside.

2 Blanch the Yunnan ham in boiling water for 30 seconds. Skim the surface, then remove the ham and set aside. Squeeze out any excess water from the mushrooms, then finely slice and discard any tough stems. Chop the bamboo shoots into small cubes.

3 Stuff the chicken with the scallion and gingerroot. Put all the ingredients except the cabbage and dipping sauce in a casserole. Bring to a boil, then lower the heat and let simmer, covered, for 1 hour. Add the cabbage and let simmer for an additional 3 minutes.

4 Remove the chicken skin before serving, then place a chunk of chicken meat in individual bowls, adding pieces of vegetable and the other meats, and pour the soup on top. Serve with the dipping sauce.

chinese mushroom soup

ingredients

SERVES 4

4 oz/115 g dried thin Chinese
   egg noodles

$1/2$ oz/15 g dried Chinese
   wood ear mushrooms,
   soaked in boiling water for
   20 minutes

2 tsp arrowroot or cornstarch

32 fl oz/1 liter/4 cups
   vegetable stock

2-inch/5-cm piece fresh
   gingerroot, peeled and
   sliced

2 tbsp dark soy sauce

2 tsp mirin or sweet sherry

1 tsp rice vinegar

4 small bok choy, each cut
   in half

salt and pepper

snipped fresh Chinese or
   ordinary chives, to garnish

method

1 Boil the noodles for 3 minutes or according to the package instructions, until soft. Drain well, rinse with cold water to stop the cooking, and set aside.

2 Strain the mushrooms through a strainer lined with a dish towel and reserve the liquid. Leave the mushrooms whole or slice them, depending on how large they are. Put the arrowroot in a wok or large pan and gradually stir in the reserved mushroom liquid. Add the vegetable stock, sliced gingerroot, soy sauce, mirin, rice vinegar, mushrooms, and bok choy and bring the mixture to a boil, stirring constantly. Lower the heat and let simmer for 15 minutes.

3 Add salt and pepper, but remember that soy sauce is salty so you might not need any salt at all—taste first. Use a slotted spoon to remove the pieces of gingerroot.

4 Divide the noodles among 4 bowls, then spoon the soup over and garnish with chives.

chinese vegetable soup

ingredients

SERVES 4–6

4 oz/115 g Napa cabbage

2 tbsp peanut oil

8 oz/225 g firm marinated
    bean curd, cut into
    $1/2$-inch/1-cm cubes

2 garlic cloves, thinly sliced

4 scallions, thinly sliced
    diagonally

1 carrot, thinly sliced

32 fl oz/1 liter/4 cups
    vegetable stock

1 tbsp Chinese rice wine

2 tbsp light soy sauce

1 tsp sugar

salt and pepper

method

1 Shred the Napa cabbage and set aside. Heat the oil in a large preheated wok or skillet over high heat. Add the bean curd cubes and stir-fry for 4–5 minutes until browned. Remove from the wok with a slotted spoon and drain on paper towels.

2 Add the garlic, scallions, and carrot to the wok and stir-fry for 2 minutes. Pour in the stock, rice wine, and soy sauce, then add the sugar and shredded Napa cabbage. Cook over medium heat, stirring, for an additional 1–2 minutes until heated through.

3 Season with salt and pepper and return the bean curd to the wok. Ladle the soup into warmed bowls and serve.

szechuan pumpkin soup

ingredients

SERVES 4–6

32 fl oz/1 liter/4 cups chicken
    stock
1 lb/450 g pumpkin, peeled
    and cut into small cubes
1 tbsp chopped preserved
    vegetables
1 tsp white pepper
4 oz/115 g any leafy green
    Chinese vegetable,
    shredded
salt (optional)

method

1 Bring the stock to a boil, then stir in the pumpkin and let simmer for 4–5 minutes.

2 Add the preserved vegetables with the pepper and stir. Finally, add the green vegetable. Season with salt, if liked. Let simmer for an additional minute and serve.

soft-wrapped pork & shrimp rolls

ingredients

MAKES 20

4 oz/115 g firm bean curd

3 tbsp vegetable or peanut oil

1 tsp finely chopped garlic

2 oz/55 g lean pork, shredded

4 oz/115 g raw shrimp,
   peeled and deveined

$1/2$ small carrot, cut into short
   thin sticks

2 oz/55 g/$1/2$ cup fresh or
   canned bamboo shoots,
   rinsed and shredded (if
   using fresh shoots, boil in
   water first for 30 minutes)

4 oz/115 g/1 cup very finely
   sliced cabbage

2 oz/55 g/$1/2$ cup snow peas,
   julienned

1-egg omelet, shredded

1 tsp salt

1 tsp light soy sauce

1 tsp Shaoxing rice wine

pinch of white pepper

20 soft spring roll skins

chili bean sauce, to serve

method

1 Slice the bean curd into thin slices horizontally and cook in 1 tablespoon of the oil until it turns golden brown. Cut into thin strips and set aside.

2 In a preheated wok or deep pan, heat the remaining oil and stir-fry the garlic until fragrant. Add the pork and stir for about 1 minute, then add the shrimp and stir for a further minute. One by one, stirring well after each addition, add the carrot, bamboo shoots, cabbage, snow peas, bean curd, and, finally, the shredded omelet. Season with the salt, light soy sauce, Shaoxing rice wine, and pepper. Stir for one more minute, then turn into a serving dish.

3 To assemble each roll, smear a skin with a little chili bean sauce and place a heaped teaspoon of the filling toward the bottom of the circle. Roll up the bottom edge to secure the filling, turn in the sides, and continue to roll up gently. Serve accompanied by a bowl of chili sauce.

pork & ginger dumplings

ingredients

MAKES ABOUT 50

1 lb/450 g/4 cups ground
pork, not too lean
1 tbsp light soy sauce
1 1/2 tsp salt
1 tsp Shaoxing rice wine
1/2 tsp sesame oil
3 1/2 oz/100 g/scant 1 cup
very finely chopped
cabbage
2 tsp minced fresh gingerroot
2 tsp finely chopped scallions
1/2 tsp white pepper
50 round wonton skins,
about 2 3/4 inches/7 cm
in diameter

ginger & garlic dipping sauce

1 tbsp soy sauce
1 tbsp vinegar
1/2 tsp sugar
1 tsp chopped gingerroot
1 tsp chopped garlic

method

1 To make the dipping sauce, stir all the ingredients together and set aside.

2 For the filling, mix the pork with the light soy sauce and 1/2 teaspoon salt. Stir carefully, always in the same direction, to create a thick paste. Add the Shaoxing and sesame oil and continue mixing in the same direction. Cover and let rest for at least 20 minutes.

3 Meanwhile, sprinkle the cabbage with the remaining salt to help draw out the water. Add the gingerroot, scallions, and white pepper and knead for at least 5 minutes into a thick paste. Combine with the filling.

4 To make the dumplings, place about 1 tablespoon of the filling in the center of each skin, holding the skin in the palm of one hand. Moisten the edges with water, then seal the edges with 2 or 3 pleats on each side and place on a lightly floured board.

5 To cook the dumplings, bring 32 fl oz/ 1 liter/4 cups water to a rolling boil in a large pan. Drop in about 20 dumplings at a time, stirring gently with a chopstick to prevent them sticking together. Cover, then bring back to a boil and cook for 2 minutes. Uncover and add about 7 fl oz/225 ml/scant 1 cup cold water. Bring back to a boil, cover and cook for an additional 2 minutes. Serve the dumplings with individual bowls of dipping sauce.

spring rolls

ingredients

MAKES 25

6 dried Chinese mushrooms,
soaked in warm water for
20 minutes

1 tbsp vegetable or peanut oil

8 oz/225 g/2 cups ground
pork

1 tsp dark soy sauce

3$\frac{1}{2}$ oz/100 g/1 cup fresh or
canned bamboo shoots,
rinsed and julienned (if
using fresh shoots, boil in
water first for 30 minutes)

pinch of salt

3$\frac{1}{2}$ oz/100 g raw shrimp,
shelled, deveined, and
chopped

8 oz/225g/generous 1$\frac{1}{2}$ cups
bean sprouts, trimmed
and coarsely chopped

1 tbsp finely chopped
scallions

25 spring roll skins

1 egg white, lightly beaten

vegetable or peanut oil, for
deep-frying

method

1 Squeeze out any excess water from the mushrooms and finely slice, discarding any tough stems.

2 In a preheated wok or deep pan, heat the tablespoon of oil and stir-fry the pork until it changes color. Add the dark soy sauce, bamboo shoots, mushrooms, and a little salt. Stir over high heat for 3 minutes.

3 Add the shrimp and cook for 2 minutes, then add the bean sprouts and cook for an additional minute. Remove from the heat and stir in the scallions. Let cool.

4 Place a tablespoon of the mixture toward the bottom of a skin. Roll once to secure the filling, then fold in the sides to create a 4-inch/10-cm piece and continue to roll up. Seal with egg white.

5 Heat enough oil for deep-frying in a wok, deep-fat fryer or large heavy-bottom pan until it reaches 350–375°F/180–190°C, or until a cube of bread browns in 30 seconds. Without overcrowding the pan, fry the rolls for about 5 minutes until golden brown and crispy. Drain well on papers towels and serve at once.

dumplings in a cold spicy sauce

ingredients

MAKES 20

20 square wheat skins

filling

1 tsp vegetable or peanut oil

7 oz/200 g/1^3/$_4$ cups ground
   pork, not too lean

1 tsp salt

^{1}/$_2$ tsp white pepper

sauce

3^1/$_2$ fl oz/100 ml/scant ^{1}/$_2$ cup
   vegetable or peanut oil

1 tbsp dried chile flakes

1 tsp sesame oil

1 tsp sugar

1 tbsp light soy sauce

^{1}/$_2$ tsp white pepper

1 tsp salt

1 garlic clove, finely chopped

method

1 To prepare the filling, heat the oil in a small pan and stir-fry the pork with the salt and pepper for 3–4 minutes, stirring to break up any meat clumps and letting the juices begin to come out.

2 To prepare the sauce, heat the oil until smoking in a wok or deep pan and pour over the chile flakes. Let cool, then stir in all the other ingredients.

3 To make the dumplings, hold a skin in the palm of one hand and place a scant teaspoon of the filling in the center. Wet the edges and fold over to create a triangle, then, with the point facing toward you at the bottom of your index finger, cross the edges behind your finger, sealing with a little water. Take the point facing toward you and turn up to form a wonton.

4 Drop the dumplings into a large pan of boiling water and cook for 5 minutes.

5 To serve, assemble 4 or 5 pieces per serving on a small plate and pour over a generous amount of the sauce.

soy chicken wings

ingredients

SERVES 3–4

9 oz/250 g chicken wings, defrosted if frozen

8 fl oz/250 ml/1 cup water

1 tbsp sliced scallion

1-inch/2.5-cm piece of fresh gingerroot, cut into 4 slices

2 tbsp light soy sauce

$^1/_2$ tsp dark soy sauce

1 star anise

1 tsp sugar

method

1 Wash and dry the chicken wings. In a small pan, bring the water to a boil, then add the chicken, scallion, and gingerroot and bring back to a boil.

2 Add the remaining ingredients, then cover and let simmer for 30 minutes.

3 Remove the chicken wings from any remaining liquid and serve hot.

whitebait with green chile

ingredients

SERVES 4

6 oz/175 g whitebait

sauce

1 tbsp vegetable or peanut oil

1 large fresh green chile

2 drops of sesame oil

1 tbsp light soy sauce

pinch of salt

pinch of sugar

1 garlic clove, finely chopped

method

1 In a large pan of boiling water, cook the fish for 30 seconds–2 minutes, or until the flesh is turning soft but not breaking up. Drain, then set aside and let cool.

2 To prepare the sauce, first heat the oil in a small pan and, when smoking, cook the chile until the skin blisters. Remove the skin and finely chop the chile. When cool, mix with all the other ingredients.

3 To serve, pour the sauce over the fish and serve immediately.

shrimp toasts

ingredients

MAKES 16

3$^1/_2$ oz/100 g raw shrimp,
    shelled, and deveined
2 egg whites
2 tbsp cornstarch
$^1/_2$ tsp sugar
pinch of salt
2 tbsp finely chopped cilantro
    leaves
2 slices day-old white bread
vegetable or peanut oil, for
    deep-frying

method

1 Pound the shrimp to a pulp in a mortar and pestle or with the base of a cleaver.

2 Mix the shrimp with one of the egg whites and 1 tablespoon of the cornstarch. Add the sugar and salt and stir in the cilantro. Mix the remaining egg white with the remaining cornstarch.

3 Remove the crusts from the bread and cut each slice into 8 triangles. Brush the top of each piece with the egg white and cornstarch mixture, then add 1 teaspoon of the shrimp mixture. Smooth the top.

4 Heat enough oil for deep-frying in a wok, deep-fat fryer, or large heavy-bottom pan until it reaches 350–375°F/180–190°C, or until a cube of bread browns in 30 seconds. Without overcrowding the wok, cook the toasts shrimp-side up for about 2 minutes. Turn and cook for an additional 2 minutes, or until beginning to turn golden brown. Drain and serve warm.

crispy crab wontons

ingredients

MAKES 24

6 oz/175 g white crabmeat,
    drained if canned and
    thawed if frozen, flaked
1³/4 oz/50 g canned water
    chestnuts, drained, rinsed
    and chopped
1 small fresh red chile,
    chopped
1 scallion, chopped
1 tbsp cornstarch
1 tsp dry sherry
1 tsp light soy sauce
¹/2 tsp lime juice
24 wonton skins
vegetable oil, for deep-frying
lime slices, to garnish

method

1 To make the filling, mix the crabmeat, water chestnuts, chile, scallion, cornstarch, sherry, soy sauce, and lime juice together in a bowl.

2 Spread the wonton skins out on a counter and spoon an equal portion of the filling into the center of each wonton skin.

3 Dampen the edges of the wonton skins with a little water and fold them in half to form triangles. Fold the 2 pointed ends in toward the center, moisten with a little water to secure, then pinch together to seal.

4 Heat the oil in a deep-fat fryer, large, heavy-bottom pan, or wok to 350–375°F/180–190°C, or until a cube of bread browns in 30 seconds. Deep-fry the wontons in batches for 2–3 minutes until golden brown and crisp (if you deep-fry too many at one time, the oil temperature will drop and they will be soggy).

5 Remove the wontons with a slotted spoon, drain on paper towels, and serve hot, garnished with lime slices.

pickled baby cucumbers

ingredients

SERVES 4

1 tbsp vegetable or peanut
   oil, for frying
14 oz/400 g baby cucumbers
18 fl oz/525 ml/generous
   2 cups white rice vinegar
1 tbsp salt
3 tbsp sugar
3 red Thai chiles, seeded and
   finely chopped

method

1 In a wok or deep pan, heat the oil and cook the cucumbers for 3–5 minutes, or until they are bright green. Drain and set aside. When cool, score the skin many times on all sides. Place in a large dish.

2 Combine the vinegar, salt, sugar, and chile and pour over the cucumbers, immersing them in the liquid. Let marinate for 24 hours, then serve cold in chunks.

lettuce wraps

ingredients

MAKES 12

3^1/$_2$ oz/100 g dried
    cellophane noodles
3 tbsp crunchy peanut butter
2 tbsp rice vinegar
1 tbsp oyster sauce
peanut or corn oil (optional)
soy sauce, to taste
4 red radishes, grated
2 carrots, peeled and coarsely
    grated
1 zucchini, coarsely grated
4 oz/115 g canned corn
    kernels, drained
12 large lettuce leaves,
    such as iceberg, rinsed
    and dried

dipping sauce

10 tbsp rice vinegar
4 tbsp clear honey
2 tbsp toasted sesame oil
1 tsp bottled chili sauce
1-inch/2.5-cm piece fresh
    gingerroot, peeled and
    very finely chopped

method

1 Put the noodles in a bowl, pour over enough lukewarm water to cover, and let soak for 20 minutes, until soft. Alternatively, follow the package instructions. Drain and rinse, then cut into 3-inch/7.5-cm lengths.

2 Beat the peanut butter, vinegar, and oyster sauce together in a large bowl, adding a little oil to lighten the mixture, if necessary. Toss with the noodles in the bowl to coat, then add soy sauce to taste. Cover and let chill until 15 minutes before you plan to serve.

3 Meanwhile, mix together the dipping sauce ingredients in a small bowl.

4 When you are ready to serve, stir the radishes, carrots, zucchini, and corn into the noodles and transfer to a serving dish. To assemble the lettuce wraps, place some noodles in a lettuce leaf and roll up the leaf to enclose the filling.

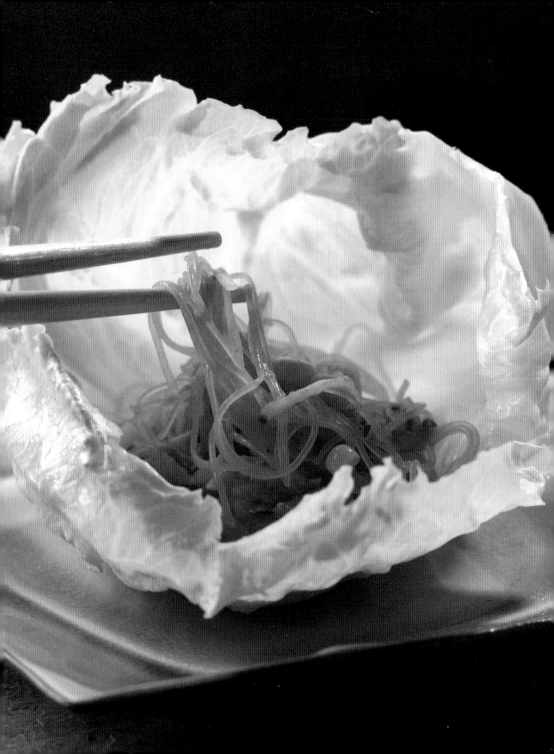

onion pancakes

ingredients

MAKES ABOUT 16

4 tbsp oil

4 tbsp finely sliced scallions

2 eggs, plus 2 egg yolks

7 oz/200 g/1^1/$_3$ cups all-
    purpose flour

1 tsp salt

14 fl oz/425 ml/1^3/$_4$ cups milk

7 fl oz/225 ml/generous
    ^{3}/$_4$ cup water

method

1 Heat 1 tablespoon of the oil in a skillet and lightly cook the scallions until beginning to soften. Remove and set aside.

2 Lightly beat the eggs, together with the egg yolks, and set aside. Sift the flour and salt into a large bowl and lightly mix in the eggs.

3 Slowly add the milk and water, beating by hand, until the batter is creamy. Stir in the remaining oil and continue to beat for a few more minutes. Finally, stir in the scallions.

4 In a nonstick skillet, pour in 1 tablespoon of the batter and cook until set, but not brown. To serve, loosely roll the pancakes and cut each one into 3 pieces.

vegetarian spring rolls

ingredients

MAKES 20

6 dried Chinese mushrooms,
    soaked in warm water for
    20 minutes

2 oz/55 g beanthread
    noodles, soaked in warm
    water for 20 minutes

2 tbsp vegetable or peanut oil

1 tbsp finely chopped fresh
    gingerroot

$3^1/_2$ oz/100 g/generous
    $^2/_3$ cup carrot, julienned

$3^1/_2$ oz/100 g/scant 1 cup
    finely shredded cabbage

1 tbsp finely sliced scallions

1 tbsp light soy sauce

3 oz/85 g soft bean curd,
    cut into small cubes

$^1/_2$ tsp salt

pinch of white pepper

pinch of sugar

20 spring roll skins

1 egg white, lightly beaten

vegetable or peanut oil,
    for deep-frying

soy sauce, for dipping

method

1 Squeeze out any excess water from the mushrooms and finely chop, discarding any tough stems. Drain the beanthread noodles and coarsely chop.

2 In a preheated wok or deep pan, heat the oil, then toss in the gingerroot and cook until fragrant. Add the mushrooms and stir for about 2 minutes. Add the carrot, cabbage, and scallions and stir-fry for 1 minute. Add the beanthread noodles and light soy sauce and stir-fry for 1 minute. Add the bean curd and cook for an additional 1 minute. Season with the salt, pepper, and sugar and mix well. Continue cooking for 1–2 minutes, or until the carrot is soft. Remove from the heat and let the mixture cool.

3 Place a scant tablespoon of the mixture toward the bottom of a skin. Roll once to secure the filling, then fold in the sides to create a 4-inch/10-cm piece and continue to roll up. Seal with egg white.

4 Heat enough oil for deep-frying in a wok, deep-fat fryer, or large heavy-bottom pan until it reaches 350–375°F/180–190°C, or until a cube of bread browns in 30 seconds. Without overcrowding the pan, cook the rolls in batches for about 5 minutes, or until golden brown and crispy. Serve with a good soy sauce for dipping.

tea-scented eggs

ingredients

SERVES 6

6 eggs

water, about 18 fl oz/525 ml/
    generous 2 cups

2 tbsp black tea leaves

method

1 Bring to a boil a pan of water deep enough to cover the eggs. Lower the eggs into the pan and cook for 10 minutes. Remove the eggs from the pan and lightly crack the shells with the back of a spoon.

2 Bring the water back to a boil and simmer the tea leaves for 5 minutes. Turn off the heat. Place the eggs in the tea and let stand until the tea has cooled.

3 Serve the eggs whole for breakfast or as part of a meal, shelled or, more traditionally, unshelled.

main dishes

One of the great joys of Chinese cooking is that it takes very little time to produce a really attractive, filling main dish. We tend, for example, to expect a casserole to need long, slow cooking, but the Xinjiang Lamb Casserole is ready to serve in less than 45 minutes—and this is the dish in this chapter with the longest cooking time! Even those recipes that require a little time for preparing the ingredients or marinating the meat or fish take only a few minutes to cook.

The main reason behind the welcome speed of Chinese dishes is the use of the wok, the most important item of equipment in an Asian kitchen. The curved shape enables the heat to be distributed quickly and evenly, and food is stir-fried for only as long as it takes to cook. Vegetables retain their vibrant color and nutritional value, while meat, which is usually cut into small pieces, is rapidly sealed and retains its juices, making it succulent and delicious. Flavorings such as ginger and chile add excitement, and sauces cloak the ingredients and ooze into the rice or noodles that invariably accompany the meal.

Fish also gets the stir-fry treatment, or is steamed or deep-fried—Steamed Sole with Black Bean Sauce can be cooked in a foil package and emerges tasting just wonderful!

marinated beef with vegetables

ingredients

SERVES 4

500 g/1 lb 2 oz rump steak, cut into thin strips

3 tbsp sesame oil

$^1/_2$ tbsp cornstarch

$^1/_2$ tbsp soy sauce

1 head of broccoli, cut into florets

2 carrots, cut into thin strips

125 g/4 oz snow peas

4 fl oz/125 ml/$^1/_2$ cup beef stock

250 g/9 oz baby spinach, shredded

freshly cooked rice or noodles, to serve

marinade

1 tbsp dry sherry

$^1/_2$ tbsp soy sauce

$^1/_2$ tbsp cornstarch

$^1/_2$ tsp superfine sugar

2 garlic cloves, chopped finely

1 tbsp sesame oil

method

1 To make the marinade, mix the sherry, soy sauce, cornstarch, sugar, garlic, and sesame oil in a bowl. Add the beef to the mixture and cover with plastic wrap. Set aside to marinate for 30 minutes, then remove the beef and discard the marinade.

2 Heat 1 tablespoon of the sesame oil in a skillet or wok. Stir-fry the beef for 2 minutes until medium-rare. Remove from the skillet and set aside.

3 Combine the cornstarch and soy sauce in a bowl and set aside. Pour the remaining 2 tablespoons of sesame oil into the skillet, add the broccoli, carrots, and snow peas and stir-fry for 2 minutes.

4 Add the stock, cover the skillet, and steam for one minute. Stir in the spinach, beef, and the cornstarch mixture. Cook until the juices boil and thicken. Serve on a bed of freshly cooked rice or noodles.

beef chop suey

ingredients

SERVES 4

1 lb/450 g ribeye or sirloin
  steak, finely sliced
1 head of broccoli, cut into
  small florets
2 tbsp vegetable or peanut oil
1 onion, finely sliced
2 celery stalks, finely sliced
  diagonally
8 oz/225g/2 cups snow peas,
  sliced in half lengthwise
2 oz/55 g/$^1/_2$ cup fresh or
  canned bamboo shoots,
  rinsed and julienned (if
  using fresh shoots, boil in
  water first for 30 minutes)
8 water chestnuts, finely sliced
8 oz/225 g/4 cups finely
  sliced mushrooms
1 tbsp oyster sauce
1 tsp salt

marinade

1 tbsp Shaoxing rice wine
pinch of white pepper
pinch of salt
1 tbsp light soy sauce
$^1/_2$ tsp sesame oil

method

1 Combine all the marinade ingredients in a bowl and marinate the beef for at least 20 minutes. Blanch the broccoli florets in a large pan of boiling water for 30 seconds. Drain and set aside.

2 In a preheated wok or deep pan, heat 1 tablespoon of the oil and stir-fry the beef until the color has changed. Remove and set aside.

3 In the clean wok or deep pan, heat the remaining oil and stir-fry the onion for 1 minute. Add the celery and broccoli and cook for 2 minutes. Add the snow peas, bamboo shoots, chestnuts, and mushrooms and cook for 1 minute. Add the beef, then season with the oyster sauce and salt and serve immediately.

hot sesame beef

ingredients

SERVES 4

1 lb 2 oz/500 g beef fillet, cut
    into thin strips

1$^{1}/_{2}$ tbsp sesame seeds

4 fl oz/125 ml/$^{1}/_{2}$ cup beef
    stock

2 tbsp soy sauce

2 tbsp grated fresh gingerroot

2 garlic cloves, chopped finely

1 tsp cornstarch

$^{1}/_{2}$ tsp chile flakes

3 tbsp sesame oil

1 large head of broccoli, cut
    into florets

1 orange bell pepper, sliced
    thinly

1 red chile, seeded and sliced
    finely

1 tbsp chili oil, to taste

1 tbsp chopped fresh cilantro,
    to garnish

method

1 Mix the beef strips with 1 tablespoon of the sesame seeds in a small bowl. In a separate bowl, whisk together the beef stock, soy sauce, gingerroot, garlic, cornstarch, and chile flakes.

2 Heat 1 tablespoon of the sesame oil in a large skillet or wok. Stir-fry the beef strips for 2–3 minutes. Remove and set aside.

3 Discard any oil left in the pan, then wipe with paper towels to remove any stray sesame seeds. Heat the remaining oil, add the broccoli, orange bell pepper, chile, and chili oil, if using, and stir-fry for 2–3 minutes. Stir in the beef stock mixture, cover, and let simmer for 2 minutes.

4 Return the beef to the skillet and let simmer until the juices thicken, stirring occasionally. Cook for another 1–2 minutes.

5 Sprinkle with the remaining sesame seeds. Serve garnished with chopped cilantro.

stir-fried beef with broccoli & ginger

ingredients

SERVES 4–6

12 oz/350 g tenderloin steak,
  cut into thin strips
6 oz/175 g head of broccoli,
  cut into florets
2 tbsp vegetable or peanut oil
1 garlic clove, finely chopped
1 tsp finely chopped fresh
  gingerroot
1 small onion, finely sliced
1 tsp salt
1 tsp light soy sauce

marinade

1 tbsp light soy sauce
1 tsp sesame oil
1 tsp Shaoxing rice wine
1 tsp sugar
pinch of white pepper

method

1 Combine the marinade ingredients in a bowl, then mix in the beef. Cover and let stand for 1 hour, basting occasionally. Blanch the broccoli in a large pan of boiling water for 30 seconds. Drain and set aside.

2 In a preheated wok or deep pan, heat 1 tablespoon of the oil and stir-fry the garlic, gingerroot, and onion for 1 minute. Add the broccoli and stir-fry for an additional minute. Remove from the wok and set aside.

3 In the clean preheated wok or deep pan, heat the remaining oil and stir-fry the beef until it has changed color. Return the broccoli mixture to the pan with the salt and light soy sauce and stir until cooked through. Serve immediately.

ginger beef with yellow bell peppers

ingredients

SERVES 4

1 lb 2 oz/500 g beef fillet, cut into 1-inch/2.5-cm cubes
2 tsp peanut oil
2 garlic cloves, crushed
2 tbsp grated fresh gingerroot
pinch of chile flakes
2 yellow bell peppers, sliced thinly
4^1/$_2$ oz/125 g baby corn
6 oz/175 g snow peas
hot noodles drizzled with sesame oil, to serve

marinade

2 tbsp soy sauce
2 tsp peanut oil
1^1/$_2$ tsp superfine sugar
1 tsp cornstarch

method

1 To make the marinade, mix the soy sauce, peanut oil, sugar, and cornstarch in a bowl. Stir in the beef cubes, then cover with plastic wrap and set aside to marinate for 30 minutes.

2 Heat the peanut oil in a skillet or wok over medium heat. Add the garlic, gingerroot, and chile flakes and cook for 30 seconds. Stir in the yellow bell peppers and baby corn, and stir-fry for 2 minutes. Add the snow peas and cook for another minute.

3 Remove the vegetables from the skillet. Put the beef cubes and marinade into the skillet and stir-fry for 3–4 minutes or until cooked to taste. Return the vegetables to the skillet, mix well, and cook until all the ingredients are heated through. Remove from the heat and serve over noodles.

xinjiang rice pot with lamb

ingredients

SERVES 6–8

2 tbsp vegetable or peanut oil

10$\frac{1}{2}$ oz/300 g lamb or mutton,
   cut into bite-size cubes

2 carrots, coarsely chopped

2 onions, coarsely chopped

1 tsp salt

1 tsp ground ginger

1 tsp Szechuan peppers,
   lightly roasted and lightly
   crushed

1 lb/450 g/generous 2 cups
   short-or medium-grain rice

30 fl oz/940 ml/3$\frac{3}{4}$ cups
   water

method

1 In a large casserole, heat the oil and stir-fry the meat for 1–2 minutes, or until the pieces are sealed on all sides. Add the carrot and onion and stir-fry until the vegetables are beginning to soften. Add the salt, ginger, and Szechuan peppers and mix well.

2 Finally, add the rice and water and bring to a boil. Cover the pan and cook over low heat for 30 minutes, or until the rice has absorbed all the water. Serve alone or as part of a meal.

xinjiang lamb casserole

ingredients

SERVES 5–6

1–2 tbsp vegetable or
   peanut oil
14 oz/400 g lamb or mutton,
   cut into bite-size cubes
1 onion, coarsely chopped
1 green bell pepper, coarsely
   chopped
1 carrot, coarsely chopped
1 turnip, coarsely chopped
2 tomatoes, coarsely chopped
1-inch/2.5-cm piece of fresh
   gingerroot, finely sliced
10 fl oz/300 ml/1^1/$_4$ cups
   water
1 tsp salt

method

1 In a preheated wok or deep pan, heat the oil and stir-fry the lamb for 1–2 minutes, or until the meat is sealed on all sides.

2 Transfer the meat to a large casserole and add all the other ingredients. Bring to a boil, then cover and let simmer over low heat for 35 minutes.

spicy szechuan pork

ingredients

SERVES 4

10 oz/280 g pork belly,
   thinly sliced

1 tbsp vegetable or peanut oil

1 tbsp chili bean sauce

1 tbsp fermented black beans,
   rinsed and lightly mashed

1 tsp sweet red bean paste
   (optional)

1 green bell pepper,
   finely sliced

1 red bell pepper, finely sliced

1 tsp sugar

1 tsp dark soy sauce

pinch of white pepper

method

1 Bring a pan of water to a boil and place the pork slices in the pan, then cover and let simmer for about 20 minutes, skimming occasionally. Let the pork cool and rest before slicing thinly.

2 In a preheated wok or deep pan, heat the oil and stir-fry the pork slices until they begin to shrink. Stir in the chili bean sauce, then add the black beans and the red bean paste, if using. Finally, toss in the bell peppers and the remaining ingredients and stir-fry for a couple of minutes.

szechuan-style pork & bell pepper

ingredients

SERVES 4

1 lb 2 oz/500 g pork
  tenderloin, cubed
2 tbsp cornstarch
3 tbsp soy sauce
1 tbsp white wine vinegar
9 fl oz/275 ml/generous 1 cup
  water
2 tbsp peanut oil
2 leeks, sliced thinly
1 red bell pepper, cut into
  thin strips
1 zucchini, cut into thin strips
1 carrot, cut into thin strips
pinch of salt
freshly cooked white and wild
  rice, to serve

marinade
1 tbsp soy sauce
pinch of chile flakes

method

1 To make the marinade, mix the soy sauce and chile flakes in a bowl. Add the pork cubes and toss to coat. Cover with plastic wrap and let stand for 30 minutes.

2 Combine the cornstarch, soy sauce, and white wine vinegar in a small bowl. Stir in the water gradually, then set aside.

3 Heat 1 tablespoon of the oil in a wok or skillet. Add the pork and marinade mixture and stir-fry for 2–3 minutes. Remove the pork from the skillet with a slotted spoon and set aside.

4 Heat the remaining oil in the skillet, add the leeks and red bell pepper, and stir-fry for 2 minutes. Then add the zucchini, carrot, and salt and stir-fry for an additional 2 minutes.

5 Stir in the pork and the cornstarch mixture and bring to a boil, stirring constantly until the sauce thickens. Remove from the heat and serve immediately with freshly cooked white and wild rice.

spareribs in a sweet-&-sour sauce

ingredients

SERVES 4

1 lb/450 g spareribs, cut into
    bite-size pieces (you or
    your butcher can cut ribs
    into pieces with a cleaver)
vegetable or peanut oil, for
    deep-frying

marinade

2 tsp light soy sauce
$1/2$ tsp salt
pinch of white pepper

sauce

3 tbsp white rice vinegar
2 tbsp sugar
1 tbsp light soy sauce
1 tbsp tomato ketchup
$1^1/2$ tbsp vegetable or
    peanut oil
1 green bell pepper,
    coarsely chopped
1 small onion,
    coarsely chopped
1 small carrot, finely sliced
$1/2$ tsp finely chopped garlic
$1/2$ tsp finely chopped
    gingerroot
$3^1/2$ oz/100 g pineapple chunks

method

1 Combine the marinade ingredients in a bowl, add the pork, and let marinate for at least 20 minutes.

2 Heat enough oil for deep-frying in a wok, deep-fat fryer, or large heavy-bottom pan until it reaches 350–375°F/180–190°C, or until a cube of bread browns in 30 seconds. Deep-fry the spareribs for 8 minutes. Drain and set aside.

3 To prepare the sauce, first mix together the vinegar, sugar, light soy sauce, and ketchup. Set aside.

4 In a preheated wok or deep pan, heat 1 tablespoon of the oil and stir-fry the bell pepper, onion, and carrot for 2 minutes. Remove and set aside.

5 In the clean preheated wok or deep pan, heat the remaining oil and stir-fry the garlic and gingerroot until fragrant. Add the vinegar mixture. Bring back to a boil and add the pineapple chunks. Finally add the spareribs and the bell pepper, onion, and carrot. Stir until warmed through and serve immediately.

sweet-&-sour chicken

ingredients

SERVES 4–6

1 lb/450 g lean chicken meat, cubed

5 tbsp vegetable or peanut oil

1/2 tsp minced garlic

1/2 tsp finely chopped fresh gingerroot

1 green bell pepper, coarsely chopped

1 onion, coarsely chopped

1 carrot, finely sliced

1 tsp sesame oil

1 tbsp finely chopped scallions

marinade

2 tsp light soy sauce

1 tsp Shaoxing rice wine

pinch of white pepper

1/2 tsp salt

dash of sesame oil

sauce

8 tbsp rice vinegar

4 tbsp sugar

2 tsp light soy sauce

6 tbsp tomato ketchup

method

1 Place all the marinade ingredients in a bowl and marinate the chicken pieces for at least 20 minutes.

2 To prepare the sauce, heat the vinegar in a pan and add the sugar, light soy sauce, and tomato ketchup. Stir to dissolve the sugar, then set aside.

3 In a preheated wok or deep pan, heat 3 tablespoons of the oil and stir-fry the chicken until it starts to turn golden brown. Remove and set aside.

4 In the clean wok or deep pan, heat the remaining oil and cook the garlic and gingerroot until fragrant. Add the vegetables and cook for 2 minutes. Add the chicken and cook for 1 minute. Finally add the sauce and sesame oil, then stir in the scallions and serve.

gong bao chicken

ingredients

SERVES 4

2 boneless chicken breasts, with or without skin, cut into $^1/_2$-inch/1-cm cubes

1 tbsp vegetable or peanut oil

10 dried red chiles or more, to taste, snipped into 2 or 3 pieces

1 tsp Szechuan peppers

3 garlic cloves, finely sliced

1-inch/2.5-cm piece of fresh gingerroot, finely sliced

1 tbsp coarsely chopped scallions, white part only

3 oz/85 g/generous $^1/_2$ cup peanuts, roasted

marinade

2 tsp light soy sauce

1 tsp Shaoxing rice wine

$^1/_2$ tsp sugar

sauce

1 tsp light soy sauce

1 tsp dark soy sauce

1 tsp black Chinese rice vinegar

a few drops of sesame oil

2 tbsp chicken stock

1 tsp sugar

method

1 Combine all the ingredients for the marinade in a bowl and marinate the chicken, covered, for at least 20 minutes. Combine all the ingredients for the sauce and set aside.

2 In a preheated wok or deep pan, heat the oil and stir-fry the chiles and peppers until crisp and fragrant. Toss in the chicken pieces. When they begin to turn white, add the garlic, gingerroot, and scallions. Stir-fry for about 5 minutes, or until the chicken is cooked.

3 Pour in the sauce, and when everything is well mixed, stir in the peanuts. Serve at once.

bang bang chicken

ingredients

SERVES 4

12 oz/350 g boneless,
  skinless chicken meat
few drops of sesame oil
2 tbsp sesame paste
1 tbsp light soy sauce
1 tbsp chicken stock
$1/2$ tsp salt
pinch of sugar
8 tbsp shredded lettuce leaves
  and 1 tbsp sesame seeds,
  roasted, to serve

method

1 Place the chicken in a pan of cold water, then bring to a boil and let simmer for 8–10 minutes. Drain and let cool a little, then cut or tear the chicken into bite-size pieces.

2 Mix together the sesame oil, sesame paste, light soy sauce, chicken stock, salt, and sugar and whisk until the sauce is thick and smooth. Toss in the chicken.

3 To serve, put the shredded lettuce on a large plate and spoon the chicken and sauce on top. Sprinkle with the sesame seeds and serve at room temperature.

chicken with cashew nuts

ingredients

SERVES 4–6

1 lb/450 g boneless chicken
    meal, cut into bite-size
    pieces
3 tbsp light soy sauce
1 tsp Shaoxing rice wine
pinch of sugar
1/2 tsp salt
3 dried Chinese mushrooms,
    soaked in warm water for
    20 minutes
2 tbsp vegetable or peanut oil
4 slices of fresh gingerroot
1 tsp finely chopped garlic
1 red bell pepper, cut into
    1-inch/2.5-cm squares
3 oz/85 g/generous 1/2 cup
    cashew nuts, roasted

method

1 Marinate the chicken in 2 tablespoons of the light soy sauce, Shaoxing, sugar, and salt for at least 20 minutes.

2 Squeeze any excess water from the mushrooms and finely slice, discarding any tough stems. Reserve the soaking water.

3 In a preheated wok or deep pan, heat 1 tablespoon of the oil. Add the gingerroot and stir-fry until fragrant. Stir in the chicken and cook for 2 minutes, or until it begins to turn brown. Before the chicken is cooked through, remove and set aside.

4 In the clean wok or deep pan, heat the remaining oil and stir-fry the garlic until fragrant. Add the mushrooms and red bell pepper and stir-fry for 1 minute. Add about 2 tablespoons of the mushroom soaking water and cook for about 2 minutes, or until the water has evaporated. Return the chicken to the wok, then add the remaining light soy sauce and the cashew nuts and stir-fry for 2 minutes, or until the chicken is thoroughly cooked through.

ginger chicken with toasted sesame seeds

ingredients

SERVES 4

1 lb 2 oz/500 g chicken
   breasts, skinned,
   cut into strips
2 tbsp peanut oil
1 leek, sliced thinly
1 head of broccoli, cut
   into small florets
2 carrots, sliced thinly
$1/2$ cauliflower, cut into
   small florets
1 tsp grated fresh gingerroot
5 tbsp white wine
2 tbsp sesame seeds
1 tbsp cornstarch
1 tbsp water
freshly cooked rice, to serve

marinade

4 tbsp soy sauce
4 tbsp water

method

1 In a medium dish, combine the soy sauce with 4 tablespoons of water. Toss and coat the chicken strips in the sauce. Cover the dish with plastic wrap and let chill in the refrigerator for 1 hour.

2 Remove the chicken from the marinade with a slotted spoon. Heat the oil in a skillet or wok and stir-fry the chicken and leek until the chicken is browned and the leek is beginning to soften. Stir in the vegetables, gingerroot, and wine. Reduce the heat, cover, and let simmer for 5 minutes.

3 Place the sesame seeds on a cookie sheet under a hot broiler. Stir them once to make sure they toast evenly. Set aside to cool.

4 In a small bowl, combine the cornstarch with 1 tablespoon of water and whisk until smooth. Gradually add the liquid to the skillet, stirring constantly until thickened.

5 Pile onto a bed of hot rice, top with the sesame seeds, and serve.

chinese crispy duck

ingredients

SERVES 4

3 tbsp soy sauce

1/4 tsp Chinese five-spice
  powder

1/4 tsp pepper and pinch
  of salt

4 duck legs or breasts,
  cut into pieces

3 tbsp vegetable oil

1 tsp dark sesame oil

1 tsp finely chopped
  gingerroot

1 large garlic clove,
  finely chopped

4 scallions, white part thickly
  sliced, green part
  shredded

2 tbsp rice wine or dry sherry

1 tbsp oyster sauce

3 whole star anise

2 tsp black peppercorns

16–20 fl oz/450–600 ml/
  2–2 1/2 cups chicken stock
  or water

6 dried shiitake mushrooms,
  soaked in warm water for
  20 minutes

8 oz/225 g canned water
  chestnuts, drained

2 tbsp cornstarch

method

1 Combine 1 tablespoon of the soy sauce, the five-spice powder, pepper, and salt and rub over the duck pieces. Place 2 1/2 tablespoons of vegetable oil in a flameproof casserole, add the duck pieces and cook until browned, then transfer to a plate and set aside.

2 Drain the fat from the casserole and wipe out. Add the sesame oil and remaining vegetable oil and heat. Add the gingerroot and garlic and cook for a few seconds. Add the sliced white scallions and cook for a few more seconds. Return the duck to the casserole. Add the rice wine, oyster sauce, star anise, peppercorns, and remaining soy sauce. Pour in enough stock to just cover the duck. Bring to a boil, cover, and let simmer gently for 1 1/2 hours, adding more stock if necessary.

3 Drain the mushrooms and squeeze dry. Slice the caps, add to the duck with the water chestnuts, and let simmer for an additional 20 minutes.

4 Mix the cornstarch with 2 tablespoons of the cooking liquid to form a smooth paste. Add to the remaining liquid, stirring, until thickened. To serve, garnish with green scallion shreds.

peking duck

ingredients

SERVES 6–10

1 duck, weighing 4 lb 8 oz/
    2 kg
56 fl oz/1.75 liters/7 cups
    boiling water
1 tbsp honey
1 tbsp Shaoxing rice wine
1 tsp white rice vinegar
1 cucumber, peeled, seeded,
    and julienned
10 scallions, white part only,
    shredded
30 Peking duck pancakes
plum or hoisin sauce, or both

method

1 To prepare the duck, massage the skin to separate it from the meat.

2 Pour the boiling water into a large pan, then add the honey, Shaoxing, and vinegar and lower in the duck. Baste for about 1 minute. Remove the duck and hang it to dry for a few hours or overnight.

3 Preheat the oven to 400°F/200°C. Place the duck on a rack above a roasting pan and roast for at least 1 hour, or until the skin is very crispy and the duck cooked through.

4 Bring the duck to the table, together with the cucumber, scallions, and pancakes, and carve off the skin first. On a pancake, arrange a little skin with some cucumber and scallion pieces. Top with a little plum or hoisin sauce, or both. Roll up and eat. Repeat the process with the lean meat.

fried fish with pine nuts

ingredients

SERVES 4–6

1/2 tsp salt

1 lb/450 g thick white fish
    fillets, cut into 1-inch/
    2.5-cm cubes

2 dried Chinese mushrooms,
    soaked in warm water
    for 20 minutes

3 tbsp vegetable or peanut oil

1-inch/2.5-cm piece of fresh
    gingerroot, finely shredded

1 tbsp chopped scallions

1 red bell pepper, cut into
    1-inch/2.5-cm squares

1 green bell pepper, cut into
    1-inch/2.5-cm squares

25 g/1 oz fresh or canned
    bamboo shoots, rinsed
    and cut into small cubes
    (if using fresh shoots,
    boil in water first for
    30 minutes)

2 tsp Shaoxing rice wine

2 tbsp pine nuts, toasted

method

1 Sprinkle the salt over the fish and set aside for 20 minutes. Squeeze out any excess water from the mushrooms and finely slice, discarding any tough stems.

2 In a preheated wok, heat 2 tablespoons of the oil and fry the fish for 3 minutes. Drain and set aside.

3 In a clean, preheated wok, heat the remaining oil and toss in the gingerroot. Stir until fragrant, then add the scallions, peppers, bamboo shoots, mushrooms, and Shaoxing and cook for 1–2 minutes.

4 Finally add the fish and stir to warm through. Sprinkle with the pine nuts and serve.

chiles stuffed with fish paste

ingredients

SERVES 4–6

8 oz/225 g white fish, minced

2 tbsp lightly beaten egg

4–6 mild red and green chiles

vegetable or peanut oil, for
    shallow-frying

2 garlic cloves, finely chopped

$1/2$ tsp fermented black beans,
    rinsed and lightly mashed

1 tbsp light soy sauce

pinch of sugar

1 tbsp water

marinade

1 tsp finely chopped fresh
    gingerroot

pinch of salt

pinch of white pepper

$1/2$ tsp vegetable or peanut oil

method

1 Combine all the ingredients for the marinade in a bowl and marinate the fish for 20 minutes. Add the egg and mix by hand to create a smooth paste.

2 To prepare the chiles, cut in half lengthwise and scoop out the seeds and loose flesh. Cut into bite-size pieces. Spread each piece of chile with about $1/2$ teaspoon of the fish paste.

3 In a preheated wok or deep pan, heat plenty of the oil and cook the chile pieces on both sides until beginning to turn golden brown. Drain and set aside.

4 Heat 1 tablespoon of the oil in a wok or deep pan and stir-fry the garlic until aromatic. Stir in the black beans and mix well. Add the light soy sauce and sugar and stir, then add the chile pieces. Add the water, then cover and let simmer over low heat for 5 minutes. Serve immediately.

whole deep-fried fish with soy & ginger

ingredients

SERVES 4–5

6 dried Chinese mushrooms, soaked in warm water for 20 minutes

3 tbsp rice vinegar

2 tbsp brown sugar

3 tbsp dark soy sauce

3-inch/7.5-cm piece fresh gingerroot, finely chopped

4 scallions, sliced diagonally

2 tsp cornstarch

2 tbsp lime juice

1 sea bass, cleaned and scaled, about 2 lb 4 oz/ 1 kg

salt and pepper

4 tbsp all-purpose flour

sunflower oil, for deep-frying

shredded Napa cabbage and radish slices, to serve

1 radish, sliced but left whole, to garnish

method

1 Drain the mushrooms, reserving 3^1/$_2$ fl oz/ 100 ml/scant ^{1}/$_2$ cup of the liquid. Cut the mushrooms into thin slices. Mix the reserved mushroom liquid with the vinegar, sugar, and soy sauce. Put in a pan with the mushrooms and bring to a boil. Reduce the heat and let simmer for 3–4 minutes. Add the gingerroot and scallions and let simmer for 1 minute.

2 Blend the cornstarch and lime juice together, stir into the pan, and cook, stirring constantly, for 1–2 minutes until the sauce thickens and clears. Set aside.

3 Season the fish inside and out with salt and pepper, then dust lightly with flour.

4 Heat 1 inch/2.5 cm of oil in a wide, heavy-bottom pan to 350–375°F/180–190°C, or until a cube of bread browns in 30 seconds. Lower the fish carefully into the oil and deep-fry on one side for 3–4 minutes until golden brown. Use 2 metal spatulas to turn the fish carefully and deep-fry on the other side for an additional 3–4 minutes, until golden brown.

5 Remove the fish, drain off the excess oil, and put on a serving plate. Reheat the sauce until boiling, then spoon it over the fish. Serve at once with shredded Napa cabbage and sliced radishes, garnished with a sliced whole radish.

five-willow fish

ingredients

SERVES 4–6

1 whole sea bass or similar,
    weighing 1 lb–1 lb 8 oz/
    450–675 g, gutted

2 tsp salt

6 tbsp vegetable or peanut oil

2 slices fresh gingerroot

2 garlic cloves, finely sliced

2 scallions, coarsely chopped

1 green bell pepper, thinly
    sliced

1 red bell pepper, thinly sliced

1 carrot, finely sliced

2 oz/55 g/$^{1}/_{2}$ cup fresh or
    canned bamboo shoots,
    rinsed and thinly sliced (if
    using fresh shoots, boil in
    water first for 30 minutes)

2 tomatoes, peeled, seeded,
    and thinly sliced

1 tbsp Shaoxing rice wine

2 tbsp white rice vinegar

1 tbsp light soy sauce

1 tbsp sugar

method

1 To prepare the fish, clean and dry it thoroughly. Score the fish on both sides with deep, diagonal cuts. Press $^{1}/_{2}$ teaspoon of the salt into the skin.

2 In a preheated wok or deep pan, heat 4 tablespoons of the oil and cook the fish for about 4 minutes on each side, or until the flesh is soft. Drain, then set aside and keep warm.

3 In a preheated wok or deep pan, heat the remaining oil and stir-fry the gingerroot, garlic, and scallions until fragrant. Toss in the vegetables with the remaining salt and stir rapidly for 2–3 minutes. Add the remaining ingredients and mix well for 2–3 minutes. Pour the sauce over the fish and serve immediately.

steamed sole with black bean sauce

ingredients

SERVES 3–4

1 sole, gutted

$^1/_2$ tsp salt

2 tsp fermented black beans, rinsed and chopped

2 tsp finely chopped garlic

1 tsp finely shredded fresh gingerroot

1 tbsp shredded scallions

1 tbsp light soy sauce

1 tsp Shaoxing rice wine

1 tsp vegetable or peanut oil

dash of sesame oil

$^1/_2$ tsp sugar

pinch of white pepper

method

1 Place the fish on a plate or create a small dish with foil.

2 Arrange all the other ingredients on top of the fish. Place in a steamer for about 10–12 minutes, or until the fish is cooked through.

deep-fried river fish with chili bean sauce

ingredients

SERVES 4–6

1 whole freshwater fish, such
   as trout or carp, weighing
   14 oz/400 g, gutted
1 heaped tbsp all-purpose
   flour
pinch of salt
3 1/2 fl oz/100 ml/scant 1/2 cup
   water
vegetable or peanut oil,
   for deep-frying

sauce
3 1/2 fl oz/100 ml/scant 1/2 cup
   vegetable or peanut oil
1 tsp dried chile flakes
1 garlic clove, finely chopped
1 tsp finely chopped fresh
   gingerroot
1 tbsp chili bean sauce
1/2 tsp white pepper
2 tsp sugar
1 tbsp white rice vinegar
1 tsp finely chopped scallions

method

1 To prepare the fish, clean and dry thoroughly. Mix together the flour, salt, and water to create a light batter. Coat the fish.

2 Heat enough oil for deep-frying in a wok, deep-fat fryer, or large heavy-bottom pan until it reaches 350–375°F/180–190°C, or until a cube of bread browns in 30 seconds. Deep-fry the fish on one side at a time until the skin is crisp and golden brown. Drain, then set aside and keep warm.

3 To make the sauce, heat all but 1 tablespoon of the oil in a small pan and, when smoking, pour over the dried chile flakes. Set aside.

4 In a preheated wok or deep pan, heat the remaining oil and stir-fry the garlic and gingerroot until fragrant. Stir in the chili bean sauce, then add the oil and chile flake mixture. Season with the pepper, sugar, and vinegar. Turn off the heat and stir in the scallions. Tip over the fish and serve immediately.

simple stir-fried scallops

ingredients

SERVES 4

1 lb/450 g scallops

2 tbsp sesame oil

1 tbsp chopped fresh cilantro

1 tbsp chopped flat-leaf
    parsley

rice noodles, to serve

sauce

2 tbsp lemon juice

2 tbsp soy sauce

1 tbsp honey

1 tbsp minced fresh
    gingerroot

1 tbsp fish sauce

1 clove garlic, peeled and
    flattened

method

1 Combine the lemon juice, soy sauce, honey, gingerroot, fish sauce, and garlic in a bowl and stir well to dissolve the honey. Add the scallops and toss to coat.

2 Heat a heavy skillet or wok over the highest heat for 3 minutes. Add the oil and heat for 30 seconds.

3 Add the scallops with their sauce and the cilantro and parsley to the skillet. Stir constantly, cooking for about 3 minutes (less time if the scallops are small). Serve immediately with rice noodles.

stir-fried scallops with asparagus

ingredients

SERVES 4

8 oz/225 g scallops

2 tsp salt

8 oz/225 g asparagus

3 tbsp vegetable or peanut oil

2 oz/55 g/$\frac{1}{2}$ cup fresh or
   canned bamboo shoots,
   rinsed and thinly sliced (if
   using fresh shoots, boil in
   water first for 30 minutes)

1 small carrot, finely sliced

4 thin slices of fresh
   gingerroot

pinch of white pepper

2 tbsp Shaoxing rice wine

2 tbsp chicken stock

1 tsp sesame oil

method

1 Sprinkle the scallops with 1 teaspoon of the salt and let stand for 20 minutes.

2 Trim the asparagus, discarding the tough ends. Cut into 2-inch/5-cm pieces and blanch in a large pan of boiling water for 30 seconds. Drain and set aside.

3 In a preheated wok, heat 1 tablespoon of the oil and cook the scallops for 30 seconds. Drain and set aside.

4 In the clean wok, heat another tablespoon of the oil and stir-fry the asparagus, bamboo shoots, and carrot for 2 minutes. Season with the remaining salt. Drain and set aside.

5 In the clean wok, heat the remaining oil, then add the gingerroot and stir-fry until fragrant. Return the scallops and vegetables to the wok and sprinkle with the pepper, Shaoxing, and stock. Cover and continue cooking for 2 minutes, then toss through the sesame oil and serve.

clams in black bean sauce

ingredients

SERVES 4

2 lb/900 g small clams

1 tbsp vegetable or peanut oil

1 tsp finely chopped fresh
gingerroot

1 tsp finely chopped garlic

1 tbsp fermented black beans,
rinsed and coarsely
chopped

2 tsp Shaoxing rice wine

1 tbsp finely chopped
scallions

1 tsp salt (optional)

method

1 Start by washing the clams thoroughly, then let them soak in clean water until it is time to drain them and toss them in the wok.

2 In a preheated wok or deep pan, heat the oil and stir-fry the gingerroot and garlic until fragrant. Add the black beans and cook for 1 minute.

3 Over high heat, add the drained clams and Shaoxing and stir-fry for 2 minutes to mix everything together. Cover and cook for about 3 minutes. Add the scallions and salt, if necessary, and serve immediately.

ginger shrimp with oyster mushrooms

ingredients

SERVES 4

about 3 tbsp vegetable oil

3 carrots, sliced thinly

12 oz/350 g oyster
  mushrooms, sliced thinly

1 large red bell pepper, sliced
  thinly

1 lb/450g large shrimp,
  shelled

2 garlic cloves, crushed

fresh cilantro leaves, to
  garnish

sauce

5 fl oz/150 ml/^{2}/$_3$ cup
  chicken stock

2 tsp sesame seeds

3 tsp grated fresh gingerroot

1 tbsp soy sauce

^{1}/$_4$ tsp hot pepper sauce

1 tsp cornstarch

method

1 In a small bowl, stir together the chicken stock, sesame seeds, gingerroot, soy sauce, hot pepper sauce, and cornstarch until well blended. Set aside.

2 In a large skillet or wok, heat 2 tablespoons of the oil. Stir-fry the carrots for 3 minutes, then remove from the skillet and set aside.

3 Add another 1 tablespoon of the oil to the skillet and fry the mushrooms for 2 minutes. Remove from the skillet and set aside.

4 Add more oil if needed and stir-fry the bell pepper with the shrimp and garlic for 3 minutes, until the shrimp turn pink and opaque.

5 Stir the sauce again and pour it into the skillet. Cook until the mixture bubbles, then return the carrots and mushrooms to the skillet. Cover and cook for an additional 2 minutes, until heated through. Serve garnished with cilantro.

shrimp, snow peas & cashew nuts

ingredients

SERVES 4

3 oz/85 g cashew nuts

3 tbsp peanut oil

4 scallions, slivered

2 celery stalks, sliced thinly

3 carrots, sliced finely

3³/₄ oz/100 g baby corn, halved

6 oz/175 g mushrooms, sliced finely

1 clove of garlic, chopped coarsely

1 lb/450 g uncooked shrimp, shelled

1 tsp cornstarch

2 tbsp soy sauce

2 fl oz/50 ml/¹/₄ cup chicken stock

8 oz/225 g savoy cabbage, shredded

6 oz/175 g snow peas

freshly cooked rice, to serve

method

1 Put a skillet or wok over medium heat, add the cashew nuts, and toast them until they begin to brown. Remove with a slotted spoon and set aside.

2 Add the oil to the skillet and heat. Add the scallions, celery, carrots, and baby corn and cook, stirring occasionally, over medium-high heat for 3–4 minutes.

3 Add the mushrooms and cook until they become brown. Mix in the garlic and shrimp, stirring until the shrimp turn pink.

4 Mix the cornstarch with the soy sauce and chicken stock until smooth. Add the liquid to the shrimp mixture and stir. Then add the savoy cabbage, snow peas, and all but a few of the cashew nuts and cook for 2 minutes.

5 Garnish with the reserved cashew nuts and serve on a bed of rice.

stir-fried fresh crab with ginger

ingredients

SERVES 4

3 tbsp vegetable or peanut oil

2 large fresh crabs, cleaned, broken into pieces and legs cracked with a cleaver

2 oz/55 g fresh gingerroot, julienned

3^1/$_2$ oz/100 g scallions, chopped into 2-inch/ 5-cm lengths

2 tbsp light soy sauce

1 tsp sugar

pinch of white pepper

method

1 In a preheated wok or deep pan, heat 2 tablespoons of the oil and cook the crab over high heat for 3–4 minutes. Remove and set aside.

2 In the clean wok or deep pan, heat the remaining oil, then toss in the gingerroot and stir until fragrant. Add the scallions, then stir in the crab pieces. Add the light soy sauce, sugar, and pepper. Cover and let simmer for 1 minute, then serve immediately.

baby squid stuffed with pork and mushrooms

ingredients

SERVES 6–8

14 oz/400 g squid

4 dried Chinese mushrooms,
    soaked in warm water
    for 20 minutes

8 oz/225 g/2 cups ground
    pork

4 water chestnuts,
    finely chopped

$1/2$ tsp sesame oil

1 tsp salt

$1/2$ tsp white pepper

dark soy sauce and 1 red
    Thai chile, chopped
    (optional), to serve

method

1 Clean the squid thoroughly, removing all the tentacles. Squeeze out any excess water from the mushrooms and finely chop, discarding any tough stems.

2 Mix the mushrooms with the pork, water chestnuts, sesame oil, salt, and pepper.

3 Force the stuffing into the squids, pressing firmly but leaving enough room to secure each one with a toothpick.

4 Steam for 15 minutes. Serve with a good soy sauce for dipping, adding the chile, if you like.

sweet chile squid

ingredients

SERVES 4

1 tbsp sesame seeds, toasted

2 tbsp sesame oil

10 oz/280 g squid, cut into
   strips

2 red bell peppers, sliced
   thinly

3 shallots, sliced thinly

3 oz/85 g mushrooms,
   sliced thinly

1 tbsp dry sherry

4 tbsp soy sauce

1 tsp sugar

1 tsp hot chile flakes,
   or to taste

1 clove of garlic, crushed

1 tsp sesame oil

freshly cooked rice, to serve

method

1 Place the sesame seeds on a cookie sheet, toast under a hot broiler, and set aside.

2 Heat 1 tablespoon of the oil in a skillet or wok over medium heat. Add the squid and cook for 2 minutes, then remove and set aside.

3 Add the other 1 tablespoon of oil to the skillet and fry the bell peppers and shallots over medium heat for 1 minute. Add the mushrooms and fry for an additional 2 minutes.

4 Return the squid to the skillet and add the sherry, soy sauce, sugar, chile flakes, and garlic, stirring thoroughly. Cook for an additional 2 minutes.

5 Sprinkle with the toasted sesame seeds, drizzle over 1 tsp sesame oil and mix. Serve on a bed of rice.

noodles & rice

Noodles and rice are the two staple carbohydrate foods of China. Rice is traditionally grown and eaten in the southern part of the country, while grains such as wheat and millet are associated with the north. The wheat is transformed into noodles, usually made with eggs, which come in all shapes and sizes and are available either fresh or dried. Rice is cooked simply as it is, but is also made into noodles, either flat ones, known as rice sticks, or very thin rice vermicelli. These are an excellent substitute for wheat-based noodles if you suffer a gluten intolerance.

There are some very poetic names for Chinese noodle recipes—Ants Climbing a Tree and Cross the Bridge Noodles are both worth making, if only to see the looks on the faces of family and friends as you serve these intriguing and very tasty dishes! Using noodles in different ways is also fun—noodle baskets are easy to master and look great filled with Chicken Chow Mein, and Sweet & Sour Vegetables on Noodle Pancakes are fabulous, too.

Fried rice is one of those dishes everyone loves, and there are several options in this section, including Fried Rice with Pork & Shrimp, a flavorful combination of meat and seafood, and Chicken Fried Rice—perfect fast food for any time of the day.

beef noodles with oyster sauce

ingredients

SERVES 4

10$^{1}/_{2}$ oz/300 g boneless
sirloin steak, thinly sliced
9 oz/250 g dried thick
Chinese egg noodles
2 tbsp peanut or corn oil
8 oz/225 g fresh asparagus
spears, woody ends cut off
and chopped
2 large garlic cloves, finely
chopped
$^{1}/_{2}$-inch/1-cm piece fresh
gingerroot, peeled and
finely chopped
$^{1}/_{2}$ red onion, thinly sliced
4 tbsp beef or vegetable stock
1$^{1}/_{2}$ tbsp rice wine
2–3 tbsp bottled oyster sauce
toasted sesame seeds,
to garnish

marinade

1 tbsp light soy sauce
1 tsp toasted sesame oil
2 tsp rice wine

method

1 To make the marinade, stir the ingredients together in a nonmetallic bowl. Stir in the steak so all the slices are coated, then set aside to marinate for at least 15 minutes.

2 Meanwhile, boil the noodles in a pan of boiling water for 4 minutes, or according to the package instructions, until soft. Drain, rinse, and drain again, then set aside.

3 When you are ready to stir-fry, heat a wok or large skillet over high heat. Add 1 tablespoon of the oil and heat. Add the asparagus and stir-fry for 1 minute. Tip the beef and marinade into the wok, standing back because it will splutter, and continue stir-frying until the beef is cooked to your taste, about 1$^{1}/_{2}$ minutes for medium. Remove the beef and asparagus from the wok and set aside.

4 Heat the remaining oil and stir-fry the garlic, gingerroot, and onion for about 1 minute, until the onion is soft. Add the stock, rice wine, and oyster sauce and bring to a boil, stirring. Return the beef and asparagus to the wok, along with the noodles. Use 2 forks to mix all the ingredients together and stir around until the noodles are hot. Sprinkle with toasted sesame seeds.

rice sticks with beef in black bean sauce

ingredients

SERVES 4–6

8 oz/225 g rump steak, finely sliced

8 oz/225 g rice sticks

2–3 tbsp vegetable or peanut oil

1 small onion, finely sliced

1 green bell pepper, finely sliced

1 red bell pepper, finely sliced

2 tbsp black bean sauce

2–3 tbsp light soy sauce

marinade

1 tbsp dark soy sauce

1 tsp Shaoxing rice wine

$1/2$ tsp sugar

$1/2$ tsp white pepper

method

1 Combine all the marinade ingredients in a bowl, add the beef, and let marinate for at least 20 minutes.

2 Cook the rice sticks according to the directions on the package. When cooked, drain and set aside.

3 In a preheated wok or deep pan, heat the oil and stir-fry the beef for 1 minute, or until the meat has changed color. Drain the meat and set aside.

4 Pour off any excess oil from the wok and stir-fry the onion and bell peppers for 1 minute. Add the black bean sauce and stir well, then pour in the light soy sauce. Toss the rice sticks in the vegetables and when fully incorporated, add the beef and stir until warmed through. Serve immediately.

ants climbing a tree

ingredients

SERVES 4

9 oz/250 g dried thick
   rice noodles
1 tbsp cornstarch
3 tbsp soy sauce
1$\frac{1}{2}$ tbsp rice wine
1$\frac{1}{2}$ tsp sugar
1$\frac{1}{2}$ tsp toasted sesame oil
12 oz/350 g/1$\frac{1}{2}$ cups lean
   fresh ground pork
1$\frac{1}{2}$ tbsp peanut or toasted
   sesame oil
2 large garlic cloves, finely
   chopped
1 large fresh red chile, or to
   taste, seeded and thinly
   sliced
3 scallions, finely chopped
finely chopped fresh cilantro
   or parsley, to garnish

method

1 Soak the rice noodles in enough lukewarm water to cover for 20 minutes, until soft, or cook according to the package instructions. Drain well and set aside.

2 Meanwhile, put the cornstarch in another large bowl, then stir in the soy sauce, rice wine, sugar, and sesame oil, stirring so that no lumps form. Add the ground pork and use your hands to toss the ingredients together without squeezing the pork; set aside to marinate for 10 minutes.

3 Heat a wok or large skillet over high heat. Add the oil and heat until it shimmers. Add the garlic, chile, and scallions and stir around for about 30 seconds. Tip in the ground pork together with any marinade left in the bowl and stir-fry for about 5 minutes, or until the pork is no longer pink. Add the noodles and use 2 forks to mix together. Sprinkle with the chopped herbs and serve.

pork lo mein

ingredients

SERVES 4–6

6 oz/175 g boneless lean
    pork, shredded
8 oz/225 g egg noodles
$1^1/2$ tbsp vegetable or
    peanut oil
2 tsp finely chopped garlic
1 tsp finely chopped fresh
    gingerroot
1 carrot, julienned
8 oz/225 g/4 cups finely
    sliced mushrooms
1 green bell pepper,
    thinly sliced
1 tsp salt
4 fl oz/125 ml/$^1/2$ cup hot
    chicken stock
7 oz/200 g/$1^1/3$ cups bean
    sprouts, trimmed
2 tbsp finely chopped
    scallions

marinade

1 tsp light soy sauce
dash of sesame oil
pinch of white pepper

method

1 Combine all the marinade ingredients in a bowl, add the pork, and let marinate for at least 20 minutes.

2 Cook the noodles according to the package instructions. When cooked, drain and set aside.

3 In a preheated wok or deep pan, heat 1 teaspoon of the oil and stir-fry the pork until it has changed color. Remove and set aside.

4 In the clean wok or pan, heat the remaining oil and stir-fry the garlic and gingerroot until fragrant. Add the carrot and cook for 1 minute, then add the mushrooms and cook for an additional 1 minute. Toss in the bell pepper and cook for 1 minute more. Add the pork, salt, and stock and heat through. Finally, toss in the noodles, followed by the bean sprouts, and stir well. Sprinkle with the scallions and serve.

singapore noodles

ingredients

SERVES 4

7 oz/200 g dried rice
vermicelli noodles
1 tbsp mild, medium, or hot
curry paste, to taste
1 tsp ground turmeric
6 tbsp water
2 tbsp peanut or corn oil
$1/2$ onion, very thinly sliced
2 large garlic cloves, thinly
sliced
3 oz/85 g head of broccoli,
cut into very small florets
3 oz/85 g green beans,
trimmed, and cut into
1-inch/2.5-cm pieces
3 oz/85 g pork fillet, cut in
half lengthwise, and then
into thin strips, or skinless,
boneless chicken breast,
thinly sliced
3 oz/85 g small cooked shelled
shrimp, thawed if frozen
2 oz/55 g Chinese cabbage or
romaine lettuce, thinly
shredded
$1/4$ Thai chile, or to taste,
seeded and thinly sliced
2 scallions, light green parts
only, thinly shredded
fresh cilantro, to garnish

method

1 Soak the noodles in enough lukewarm water to cover for 20 minutes, or according to the package instructions, until soft. Drain and set aside until required. While the noodles are soaking, put the curry paste and turmeric in a small bowl and stir in 4 tablespoons of the water, then set aside.

2 Heat a wok or large skillet over high heat. Add the oil and heat until it shimmers. Add the onion and garlic and stir-fry for 1 minute, or until the onion softens. Add the broccoli florets and beans to the wok with the remaining 2 tablespoons water and continue stir-frying for 2 minutes. Add the pork and stir-fry for 1 more minute. Add the shrimp, cabbage, and chile to the wok and continue stir-frying for an additional 2 minutes, until the meat is cooked through and the vegetables are tender, but still with a little bite. Scoop out of the wok and keep warm.

3 Add the scallions, noodles, and curry paste mixture to the wok. Use 2 forks to mix the noodles and onions together, and continue stir-frying for about 2 minutes, until the noodles are hot and have picked up a dark golden color from the turmeric. Return the other ingredients to the wok and continue stir-frying and mixing for 1 minute. Garnish with fresh cilantro.

sour-&-spicy pork

ingredients

SERVES 4

2 oz/55 g dried Chinese
   cloud ear mushrooms,
   soaked in boiling water for
   20 minutes
3¹/₂ oz/100 g baby corn,
   halved lengthwise
2 tbsp honey
1 tbsp tamarind paste
4 tbsp boiling water
2 tbsp dark soy sauce
1 tbsp rice vinegar
2 tbsp peanut or corn oil
1 large garlic clove, very
   finely chopped
¹/₂-inch/1-cm piece fresh
   gingerroot, peeled and
   very finely chopped
¹/₂ tsp dried red pepper
   flakes, or to taste
12 oz/350 g pork fillet,
   thinly sliced
4 scallions, thickly sliced
   diagonally
1 green bell pepper, cored,
   seeded, and sliced
9 oz/250 g fresh Hokkien
   noodles
chopped fresh cilantro,
   to garnish

method

1 Drain the mushrooms well, then cut off and discard any thick stems, and slice the cups if they are large. Meanwhile, bring a large pan of lightly salted water to a boil, add the baby corn, and blanch for 3 minutes. Drain the corn and run them under cold running water to stop the cooking, then set aside.

2 Put the honey and tamarind paste in a small bowl and stir in the water, stirring until the paste dissolves. Then stir in the soy sauce and rice vinegar and set aside.

3 Heat a wok or large skillet over high heat. Add 1 tablespoon of the oil and heat until it shimmers. Add the garlic, gingerroot, and red pepper flakes and stir-fry for about 30 seconds. Add the pork and continue stir-frying for 2 minutes.

4 Add the remaining oil to the wok and heat. Add the scallions, bell pepper, mushrooms, and baby corn, along with the tamarind mixture, and stir-fry for an additional 2–3 minutes, until the pork is cooked through and the vegetables are tender, but still firm to the bite. Add the noodles and use 2 forks to mix all the ingredients together. When the noodles and sauce are hot, sprinkle with cilantro.

hoisin pork with garlic noodles

ingredients

SERVES 4

9 oz/250 g dried thick Chinese
   egg noodles, or Chinese
   whole wheat egg noodles
1 lb/450 g pork fillet, thinly
   sliced
1 tsp sugar
1 tbsp peanut or corn oil
4 tbsp rice vinegar
4 tbsp white wine vinegar
4 tbsp bottled hoisin sauce
2 scallions, sliced diagonally
about 2 tbsp garlic-flavored
   corn oil
2 large garlic cloves, thinly
   sliced

method

1 Cook the noodles in a pan of boiling water for 3 minutes, or according to the package instructions, until soft. Drain well, rinse under cold water to stop the cooking, and drain again, then set aside.

2 Meanwhile, sprinkle the pork slices with the sugar and use your hands to toss together. Heat a wok or large skillet over high heat. Add the oil and heat until it shimmers. Add the pork and stir-fry for about 3 minutes, until the pork is cooked through and is no longer pink. Use a slotted spoon to remove the pork from the wok and keep warm. Add both vinegars to the wok and boil until they are reduced to about 5 tablespoons. Pour in the hoisin sauce with the scallions and let bubble until reduced by half. Add to the pork and stir together.

3 Quickly wipe out the wok and reheat. Add the garlic-flavored oil and heat until it shimmers. Add the garlic slices and stir round for about 30 seconds, until they are golden and crisp, then use a slotted spoon to scoop them out of the wok and set aside.

4 Add the noodles to the wok and stir to warm through. Divide the noodles among 4 plates, top with the pork and onion mixture, and sprinkle with cooked garlic slices.

fried rice with pork & shrimp

ingredients

SERVES 4

3 tsp vegetable or peanut oil

1 egg, lightly beaten

3^1/$_2$ oz/100 g raw shrimp,
  shelled, deveined and
  cut into 2 pieces

3^1/$_2$ oz/100 g cha siu (roast
  honeyed pork),
  finely chopped

2 tbsp finely chopped
  scallions

7 oz/200 g cooked rice, chilled

1 tsp salt

method

1 In a preheated wok or deep pan, heat 1 teaspoon of the oil and pour in the egg. Cook until scrambled. Remove and set aside.

2 Add the remaining oil and stir-fry the shrimp, cha siu, and scallions for about 2 minutes. Add the rice and salt, breaking up the rice into grains, and cook for an additional 2 minutes. Finally, stir in the cooked egg. Serve immediately.

peking duck salad

ingredients

SERVES 4

$^1/_2$ Peking duck (see page
86), or 2 duck breasts
1 lb/450 g fresh Hokkien
noodles
5 tbsp bottled hoisin sauce
5 tbsp bottled plum sauce
1 small cucumber
4 scallions, sliced diagonally

method

1 Roast and cool the duck breasts, if using.
Remove the crisp skin from the Peking duck
or roasted duck breasts and cut it into thin
strips, then slice the meat and set both
aside separately.

2 Rinse the noodles under lukewarm water to
separate them, then let them drain. Meanwhile,
mix the hoisin and plum sauces together in a
large bowl and add the noodles after any
excess water has dripped off. Add the duck
skin to the bowl and stir together.

3 Cut the cucumber in half lengthwise, then
use a teaspoon to scoop out the seeds. Cut
into half-moon slices and add to the noodles.
Add the scallions to the bowl. Use your hands
to mix all the ingredients together so they are
coated with the sauce.

4 Transfer the noodles to a large platter and
arrange the duck meat on top.

chicken fried rice

ingredients

SERVES 4

$1/2$ tbsp sesame oil

6 shallots, peeled and cut into fourths

1 lb/450g cooked, cubed chicken meat

3 tbsp soy sauce

2 carrots, diced

1 stalk celery, diced

1 red bell pepper, diced

6 oz/175g fresh peas

$3^1/2$ oz/100 g canned corn

$9^1/2$ oz/275 g cooked long-grain rice

2 large eggs, scrambled

method

1 Heat the oil in a large skillet over medium heat. Add the shallots and fry until soft, then add the chicken and 2 tablespoons of the soy sauce and stir-fry for 5–6 minutes.

2 Stir in the carrots, celery, red bell pepper, peas, and corn and stir-fry for an additional 5 minutes. Add the rice and stir thoroughly.

3 Finally, stir in the scrambled eggs and the remaining tablespoon of soy sauce. Serve immediately.

sweet-&-sour noodles with chicken

ingredients

SERVES 4

9 oz/250 g dried medium
    Chinese egg noodles
2 tbsp peanut or corn oil
1 onion, thinly sliced
4 boneless chicken thighs,
    skinned and cut into
    thin strips
1 carrot, peeled and cut into
    thin half-moon slices
1 red bell pepper, cored,
    seeded, and finely chopped
$3^1/_2$ oz/100 g canned bamboo
    shoots, drained weight
2 oz/55 g/scant $^1/_2$ cup
    cashew nuts

sweet-&-sour sauce

4 fl oz/125 ml/$^1/_2$ cup water
$1^1/_2$ teaspoons arrowroot
4 tbsp rice vinegar
3 tbsp brown sugar
2 tsp dark soy sauce
2 tsp tomato paste
2 large garlic cloves, very
    finely chopped
$^1/_2$-inch/1-cm piece fresh
    gingerroot, peeled and
    very finely chopped
pinch of salt

method

1 Cook the noodles in a large pan of boiling water for 3 minutes, or according to the package instructions, until soft. Drain, rinse, and drain again, then set aside.

2 Meanwhile, to make the sauce, stir half the water into the arrowroot, and set aside. Stir the remaining sauce ingredients and the remaining water together in a small pan and bring to a boil. Stir in the arrowroot mixture and continue boiling until the sauce becomes clear, glossy, and thick. Remove from the heat and set aside.

3 Heat a wok or large skillet over high heat. Add the oil and heat it until it shimmers. Add the onion and stir-fry for 1 minute. Stir in the chicken, carrot, and bell pepper and continue stir-frying for about 3 minutes, or until the chicken is cooked through. Add the bamboo shoots and cashew nuts and stir them round to lightly brown the nuts. Stir the sauce into the wok and heat until it starts to bubble. Add the noodles and use 2 forks to mix them with the chicken and vegetables.

chicken & green vegetables

ingredients

SERVES 4

9 oz/250 g dried medium Chinese egg noodles

2 tbsp peanut or corn oil

1 large garlic clove, crushed

1 fresh green chile, seeded and sliced

1 tbsp Chinese five-spice powder

2 skinless, boneless chicken breasts, cut into thin strips

2 green bell peppers, cored, seeded, and sliced

4 oz/115 g head of broccoli, cut into small florets

2 oz/55 g green beans, trimmed and cut into 1^1/$_2$-inch/4-cm pieces

5 tbsp vegetable or chicken stock

2 tbsp bottled oyster sauce

2 tbsp soy sauce

1 tbsp rice wine or dry sherry

3^1/$_2$ oz/100 g/^{2}/$_3$ cup bean sprouts

method

1 Cook the noodles in a pan of boiling water for 4 minutes, or according to the package instructions, until soft. Drain, rinse, and drain again, then set aside.

2 Heat a wok or large skillet over high heat. Add 1 tablespoon of the oil and heat until it shimmers. Add the garlic, chile, and five-spice powder and stir-fry for about 30 seconds. Add the chicken and stir-fry for 3 minutes, or until it is cooked through. Use a slotted spoon to remove the chicken from the wok and set aside.

3 Add the remaining oil to the wok and heat until it shimmers. Add the bell peppers, broccoli, and beans and stir-fry for about 2 minutes. Stir in the stock, oyster sauce, soy sauce, and rice wine and return the chicken to the wok. Continue stir-frying for about 1 minute, until the chicken is reheated and the vegetables are tender but still firm to the bite. Add the noodles and bean sprouts and use 2 forks to mix all the ingredients together.

chicken chow mein

ingredients

SERVES 4

9 oz/250 g dried medium
   Chinese egg noodles

2 tbsp sunflower oil

10 oz/280 g cooked chicken
   breasts, shredded

1 garlic clove, finely chopped

1 red bell pepper, seeded and
   thinly sliced

3¹/₂ oz/100 g shiitake
   mushrooms, sliced

6 scallions, sliced

3¹/₂ oz/100 g/³/₄ cup bean
   sprouts

3 tbsp soy sauce

1 tbsp sesame oil

method

1 Place the egg noodles in a large bowl or dish and break them up slightly. Pour enough boiling water over the noodles to cover and let stand while preparing the other ingredients.

2 Preheat a wok over medium heat. Add the sunflower oil and swirl it around to coat the sides of the wok. When the oil is hot, add the shredded chicken, garlic, bell pepper, mushrooms, scallions, and bean sprouts to the wok and stir-fry for about 5 minutes.

3 Drain the noodles thoroughly then add them to the wok, toss well, and stir-fry for an additional 5 minutes. Drizzle over the soy sauce and sesame oil and toss until thoroughly combined.

4 Transfer to warmed serving bowls and serve immediately.

chicken chow mein baskets

ingredients

SERVES 4

9 oz/250 g fresh thin or
   medium Chinese egg
   noodles
peanut or corn oil, for
   deep-frying
6 tbsp water
3 tbsp soy sauce
1 tbsp cornstarch
3 tbsp peanut or corn oil
4 boneless chicken thighs,
   skinned and chopped
1-inch/2.5-cm piece fresh
   gingerroot, peeled and
   finely chopped
2 large garlic cloves, crushed
2 celery stalks, thinly sliced
3¹/2 oz/100 g white
   mushrooms, wiped and
   thinly sliced

method

1 Dip a large wire strainer in oil, then line it completely and evenly with one fourth of the tangled noodles. Dip a smaller wire strainer in oil, then position it inside the larger strainer. Heat 4 inches/10 cm of oil in a wok to 350–375°F/180–190°C, or until a cube of bread browns in 30 seconds. Lower the strainers into the oil and deep-fry the noodles for 2–3 minutes, until golden brown. Remove from the oil and drain on paper towels. Carefully remove the small strainer and remove the noodle basket. Repeat to make 3 more baskets. Let cool.

2 Stir the water and soy sauce into the cornstarch in a small bowl and set aside.

3 Heat a wok or large skillet over high heat. Add 2 tablespoons of the oil and heat until it shimmers. Add the chicken and stir-fry for about 3 minutes, or until it is cooked through. Remove the chicken from the wok.

4 Add the remaining oil, then add the gingerroot, garlic, and celery and stir-fry for 2 minutes. Add the mushrooms and continue stir-frying for 2 minutes. Remove the vegetables and add them to the chicken.

5 Pour the cornstarch mixture into the wok and bring to a boil, stirring until it thickens. Return the chicken and vegetables to the wok and reheat in the sauce. Divide the chicken mixture among the noodle baskets to serve.

chicken-sesame salad

ingredients

SERVES 4

7 oz/200 g dried thick
  Chinese egg noodles
3^1/$_2$ oz/100 g snow peas
2 celery stalks
4 cooked skinless chicken
  thighs

sesame dressing

3 tbsp dark soy sauce
3 tbsp Chinese sesame paste
^{1}/$_2$ tbsp bottled hoisin sauce
^{1}/$_2$ tbsp sugar
^{1}/$_2$–1 tbsp bottled sweet chili
  sauce, to taste
1 tsp rice wine
^{1}/$_2$ tbsp boiling water

method

1 To make the dressing, whisk the soy sauce, sesame paste, hoisin sauce, sugar, chili sauce, and rice wine together, then whisk in the boiling water and continue whisking until the sugar dissolves. Let the dressing stand until it is cool, then cover and let chill until required.

2 Meanwhile, cook the noodles in boiling water for 5 minutes, or according to the package instructions, until soft. Drain, rinse with cold water to stop the cooking, and drain again. Set aside.

3 Use a small, sharp knife to slice the snow peas into thin, lengthwise strips, and cut the celery into thin strips. Use your hands to pull the chicken into thin shreds. If you aren't serving the salad straightaway, cover the chicken and vegetables and let chill.

4 When you are ready to serve, put the noodles, snow peas, celery, and chicken in a large bowl. Toss together so all the ingredients are mixed and pour the dressing on top.

cross the bridge noodles

ingredients

SERVES 4

10^1/$_2$ oz/300 g thin Chinese egg or rice sticks

7 oz/200 g choi sum or similar green vegetable

66 fl oz/2 liters/8 cups chicken stock

^{1}/$_2$-inch/1-cm piece of fresh gingerroot, peeled

1–2 tsp salt

1 tsp sugar

1 boneless, skinless chicken breast, finely sliced diagonally

7 oz/200 g white fish fillet, finely sliced diagonally

1 tbsp light soy sauce

method

1 Cook the noodles according to the directions on the package. When cooked, rinse under cold water and set aside. Blanch the choi sum in a large pan of boiling water for 30 seconds. Rinse under cold water and set aside.

2 In a large pan, bring the chicken stock to a boil, then add the gingerroot, 1 teaspoon of the salt, and the sugar and skim the surface. Add the chicken and cook for about 4 minutes, then add the fish slices and simmer for an additional 4 minutes, or until the fish and chicken are cooked through.

3 Add the noodles and choi sum with the light soy sauce and bring back to a boil. Taste and adjust the seasoning if necessary. Serve immediately in large individual noodle bowls.

congee with fish fillet

ingredients

SERVES 6–8

8 oz/225 g/generous 1 cup
   short-grain rice

96 fl oz/3 liters/12 cups water

7 oz/200 g firm white fish
   fillet, flaked

2 tsp salt

$^1/_2$ tsp white pepper

6 oz/175 g lettuce, finely
   shredded

2 tbsp finely shredded
   scallions

2 tbsp finely shredded fresh
   gingerroot

3 tbsp light soy sauce,
   to serve

method

1 Wash the rice and place in a large pan with the water. Cover, and cook for about 2 hours, stirring regularly.

2 Add the fish fillet, salt, and pepper. Stir well, then return to a boil and cook for a couple more minutes.

3 To serve, divide the lettuce, scallions, and gingerroot among large individual bowls. Pour the congee on top. Finally, sprinkle with 1–2 teaspoons of good-quality soy sauce.

seafood chow mein

ingredients

SERVES 4

3 oz/85 g squid, cleaned

3–4 fresh scallops

3 oz/85 g raw shrimp, shelled

1/2 egg white, lightly beaten

2 tsp cornstarch, mixed to a
    paste with 2 1/2 tsp water

9 1/2 oz/275 g dried thin
    Chinese egg noodles

5–6 tbsp vegetable oil

2 tbsp light soy sauce

2 oz/55 g snow peas

1/2 tsp salt

1/2 tsp sugar

1 tsp Chinese rice wine

2 scallions, shredded finely

a few drops of sesame oil

method

1 Open up the squid and score the inside in a criss-cross pattern, then cut into pieces about 1 inch/2.5 cm square. Soak the squid in a bowl of boiling water until all the pieces curl up. Rinse in cold water and drain.

2 Cut each scallop into 3–4 slices. Cut the shrimp in half lengthwise if large. Mix the scallops and shrimp with the egg white and cornstarch paste.

3 Cook the noodles in boiling water according to the package instructions, then drain and rinse under cold water. Drain well, then toss with about 1 tablespoon of the oil.

4 Heat 3 tablespoons of the oil in a preheated wok. Add the noodles and 1 tablespoon of the soy sauce and stir-fry for 2–3 minutes. Remove to a large serving dish.

5 Heat the remaining oil in the wok and add the snow peas and seafood. Stir-fry for about 2 minutes, then add the salt, sugar, rice wine, remaining soy sauce, and about half the scallions. Blend well and add a little water if necessary. Pour the seafood mixture on top of the noodles and sprinkle with sesame oil. Garnish with the remaining scallions and serve immediately.

crab fried rice

ingredients

SERVES 4

$5^1/2$ oz/150 g/$^3/4$ cup
   long-grain rice

2 tbsp peanut oil

$4^1/2$ oz/125 g canned white
   crab meat, drained

1 leek, sliced

$5^1/2$ oz/150 g/1 cup bean
   sprouts

2 eggs, beaten

1 tbsp light soy sauce

2 tsp lime juice

1 tsp sesame oil

salt

sliced lime, to garnish

method

1 Cook the rice in a pan of lightly salted boiling water for 15 minutes. Drain, rinse under cold running water, and drain again.

2 Heat the oil in a preheated wok or large, heavy-based skillet until it is really hot. Add the crab meat, leek, and bean sprouts to the wok or skillet and stir-fry for 2–3 minutes. Remove the mixture with a slotted spoon and reserve.

3 Add the eggs to the wok and cook, stirring occasionally, for 2–3 minutes, until they begin to set. Stir the rice and the crab meat mixture into the eggs.

4 Add the soy sauce and lime juice to the mixture in the wok. Cook for 1 minute, stirring to combine. Sprinkle with the sesame oil and toss lightly to mix.

5 Transfer the crab fried rice to a serving dish, garnish with the sliced lime and serve at once.

chinese shrimp salad

ingredients

SERVES 4

9 oz/250 g dried thin Chinese
   egg noodles
3 tbsp sunflower oil
1 tbsp sesame oil
1 tbsp sesame seeds
6 oz/175 g/generous 1 cup
   bean sprouts
1 mango, peeled, pitted,
   and sliced
6 scallions, sliced
$2^3/_4$ oz/75 g radishes, sliced
12 oz/350 g cooked shelled
   shrimp
2 tbsp light soy sauce
1 tbsp sherry

method

1 Put the noodles in a large, heatproof bowl and pour over enough boiling water to cover. Let stand for 10 minutes, then drain thoroughly and pat dry with paper towels.

2 Heat the sunflower oil in a large, preheated wok. Add the noodles and stir-fry for 5 minutes, tossing frequently.

3 Remove the wok from the heat and add the sesame oil, sesame seeds, and bean sprouts, tossing to mix well.

4 Mix the mango, scallions, radishes, shrimp, soy sauce, and sherry together in a separate bowl. Toss the shrimp mixture with the noodles. Alternatively, arrange the noodles around the edge of a serving plate and pile the shrimp mixture into the center. Serve at once.

egg fu yung

ingredients

SERVES 4–6

2 eggs

$^1\!/_2$ tsp salt

pinch of white pepper

1 tsp melted butter

2 tbsp vegetable or peanut oil

1 tsp finely chopped garlic

1 small onion, finely sliced

1 green bell pepper,
    finely sliced

1 lb/450 g cooked rice,
    chilled

1 tbsp light soy sauce

1 tbsp finely chopped
    scallions

5 oz/150 g/1 cup bean
    sprouts, trimmed

2 drops of sesame oil

method

1 Beat the eggs with the salt and pepper. Heat the butter in a pan and pour in the eggs. Cook as an omelet, until set, then remove from the pan and cut into slivers.

2 In a preheated wok or deep pan, heat the oil and stir-fry the garlic until fragrant. Add the onion and stir-fry for 1 minute, then add the green bell pepper and stir-fry for an additional 1 minute. Stir in the rice and when the grains are separated, stir in the light soy sauce and cook for 1 minute.

3 Add the scallions and egg strips and stir well, then finally add the bean sprouts and sesame oil. Stir-fry for 1 minute and serve.

szechuan noodles

ingredients

SERVES 4

1 large carrot

9 oz/250 g dried thick
　Chinese egg noodles

2 tbsp peanut or corn oil

2 large garlic cloves, very
　finely chopped

1 large red onion, cut in half
　and thinly sliced

$1/2$ cup vegetable stock or water

2 tbsp bottled chili bean sauce

2 tbsp Chinese sesame paste

1 tbsp dried Szechuan
　peppercorns, roasted
　and ground

1 tsp light soy sauce

2 small bok choy or other
　Chinese cabbage, cut
　into fourths

method

1 Peel the carrot and cut off both ends, then grate it lengthwise on the coarsest side of a grater to make long, thin strips. Set the carrot strips aside.

2 Cook the noodles in a pan of boiling water for 4 minutes, or according to the package instructions, until soft. Drain and rinse with cold water to stop the cooking, then set aside.

3 Heat a wok or large skillet over high heat. Add the oil and heat until it shimmers. Add the garlic and onion and stir-fry for 1 minute. Add the vegetable stock, chili bean sauce, sesame paste, ground Szechuan peppercorns, and soy sauce and bring to a boil, stirring to blend the ingredients together. Add the bok choy fourths and carrot strips and continue stir-frying for 1–2 minutes, until they are just wilted. Add the noodles and continue stir-frying, using 2 forks to mix all the ingredients together. Serve the noodles when they are hot.

hot-&-sour noodle salad

ingredients

SERVES 4

12 oz/350 g dried rice
    vermicelli noodles

4 tbsp sesame oil

3 tbsp soy sauce

juice of 2 limes

1 tsp sugar

4 scallions, finely sliced

1–2 tsp hot chili sauce

2 tbsp chopped fresh cilantro

method

1 Prepare the noodles according to the package instructions. Drain, put in a bowl, and toss with half the oil.

2 Mix the remaining oil, soy sauce, lime juice, sugar, scallions, and chili sauce together in a bowl. Stir into the noodles.

3 Stir in the cilantro and serve.

sweet-&-sour vegetables on noodle pancakes

ingredients

SERVES 4

4 oz/115 g dried thin
    cellophane noodles
6 eggs
4 scallions, sliced diagonally
salt and pepper
2^1/$_2$ tbsp peanut or corn oil
2 lb/900 g selection of
    vegetables, such as carrots,
    baby corn, cauliflower,
    broccoli, snow peas, and
    onions, peeled as
    necessary and chopped
    into same-size pieces
3^1/$_2$ oz/100 g canned bamboo
    shoots, drained
7 oz/200 g/scant 1 cup
    bottled sweet-and-sour
    sauce

method

1 Soak the noodles in enough lukewarm water to cover and let stand for 20 minutes, or according to the package instructions, until soft. Drain them well and use scissors to cut into 3-inch/7.5-cm pieces, then set aside.

2 Beat the eggs, then stir in the noodles, the scallions, salt, and pepper. Heat an 8-inch/20-cm skillet over high heat. Add 1 tablespoon oil and swirl it around. Pour in a fourth of the egg mixture and tilt the skillet so it covers the bottom. Lower the heat to medium and cook for 1 minute, or until the thin pancake is set. Flip it over and add a little extra oil, if necessary. Continue cooking until beginning to color. Keep warm in a low oven while you make 3 more pancakes.

3 After you've made 4 pancakes, heat a wok or large, heavy-bottom skillet over high heat. Add 1^1/$_2$ tablespoons oil and heat until it shimmers. Add the thickest vegetables, such as carrots, first and stir-fry for 30 seconds. Gradually add the remaining vegetables and bamboo shoots. Stir in the sauce and stir-fry until all the vegetables are tender and the sauce is hot. Spoon the vegetables and sauce over the pancakes.

egg-fried rice with peas

ingredients

SERVES 4

5^1/$_2$ oz/150 g long-grain rice

3 eggs, beaten

2 tbsp vegetable oil

2 garlic cloves, crushed

4 scallions, chopped

4^1/$_2$ oz/125 g cooked peas

1 tbsp light soy sauce

pinch of salt

shredded scallions, to garnish

method

1 Cook the rice in a pan of boiling water for 10–12 minutes until almost cooked, but not soft. Drain well, rinse under cold running water and drain thoroughly.

2 Place the beaten eggs in a pan and cook over low heat, stirring constantly, until softly scrambled. Remove the pan from the heat and set aside.

3 Preheat a wok over medium heat. Add the oil and swirl it around to coat the sides of the wok. When the oil is hot, add the garlic, scallions, and peas and sauté, stirring occasionally, for 1–2 minutes.

4 Stir the rice into the mixture in the wok, mixing to combine. Add the eggs, soy sauce, and salt to the wok and stir to mix in the eggs thoroughly.

5 Transfer to serving dishes and serve garnished with the shredded scallions.

spicy bean curd

ingredients

SERVES 4

9 oz/250 g firm bean curd, rinsed and drained thoroughly and cut into $1/2$-inch/1-cm cubes

4 tbsp peanut oil

1 tbsp grated fresh gingerroot

3 garlic cloves, crushed

4 scallions, sliced thinly

1 head of broccoli, cut into florets

1 carrot, cut into batons

1 yellow bell pepper, sliced thinly

9 oz/250 g shiitake mushrooms, sliced thinly

steamed rice, to serve (see page 216)

marinade

5 tbsp vegetable stock

2 tsp cornstarch

2 tbsp soy sauce

1 tbsp superfine sugar

pinch of chile flakes

method

1 Combine all the ingredients for the marinade in a large bowl. Add the bean curd and toss well to cover in the marinade. Set aside to marinate for 20 minutes.

2 In a large skillet or wok, heat 2 tablespoons of the peanut oil and stir-fry the bean curd with its marinade until brown and crispy. Remove from the skillet and set aside.

3 Heat the remaining 2 tablespoons of peanut oil in the skillet and stir-fry the gingerroot, garlic, and scallions for 30 seconds. Add the broccoli, carrot, yellow bell pepper, and mushrooms to the skillet and cook for 5–6 minutes. Return the bean curd to the skillet and stir-fry to reheat. Serve immediately over steamed rice.

a firepot of mushrooms & bean curd

ingredients

SERVES 4

2 oz/55 g dried Chinese
 mushrooms
4 oz/115 g firm bean curd,
 drained
2 tbsp bottled sweet chili sauce
2 tbsp peanut or corn oil
2 large garlic cloves, chopped
1/2-inch/1-cm piece fresh
 gingerroot, peeled and
 finely chopped
1 red onion, sliced
1/2 tbsp Szechuan peppercorns,
 lightly crushed
2 oz/55 g canned straw
 mushrooms, drained
 weight, rinsed
vegetable stock
1 star anise
pinch of sugar
soy sauce, to taste
4 oz/115 g dried thin
 cellophane noodles

method

1 Soak the mushrooms in enough boiling water to cover for 20 minutes, or until soft. Cut the bean curd into bite-size chunks and coat with the chili sauce, then let marinate.

2 Just before you are ready to start cooking, strain the soaked mushrooms through a strainer lined with a paper towel, reserving the soaking liquid. Heat the oil in a medium-size ovenproof casserole or large skillet with a lid. Add the garlic and gingerroot and stir them around for 30 seconds. Add the onion and peppercorns and keep stirring until the onion is almost tender. Add the bean curd, the soaked mushrooms, and canned mushrooms and stir carefully so the bean curd doesn't break up.

3 Add the reserved mushroom soaking liquid to the wok with just enough vegetable stock or water to cover. Stir in the star anise and a pinch of sugar with several dashes of soy sauce. Bring to a boil, then reduce the heat to the lowest setting, cover, and let simmer for 5 minutes. Add the noodles, re-cover and simmer for an additional 5 minutes, or until the noodles are tender. The noodles should be covered with liquid, so add extra stock at this point, if necessary. Use a fork or wooden spoon to stir the noodles into the other ingredients. Add more soy sauce, if liked.

vegetables &
side dishes

Even if you aren't cooking a full Chinese meal, it's worth cooking your vegetables Chinese-style—they are nutritious and absolutely bursting with flavor, color, and interest. The wok is used to great effect here, too, and vegetables cook so rapidly that they retain their texture to perfection. If you don't have a wok, a deep pan or heavy-bottom skillet can be used instead. Another item of equipment you might consider is a little "claypot" with a lid and a glazed inside, which is excellent for braising— Braised Straw Mushrooms simply melt in the mouth.

Not all vegetable dishes are vegetarian—for example, Chunky Potatoes with Cilantro Leaves, for example, includes a little pork, and it is not unusual to use chicken stock in the cooking or to add oyster sauce for flavor. If you are looking for a vegetarian main dish, Sweet-&-Sour Vegetables with Cashew Nuts and Vegetable & Coconut Curry are delicious options.

The Chinese are very good at eating their greens—and very cook at cooking them, too. Stir-fried Green Beans with Red Bell Pepper, Broccoli & Snow Pea Stir-fry, Stir-fried Chinese Greens, and Garlic Spinach Stir-fry are irresistibly tempting and will convert anyone who was ever put off by overcooked vegetables!

chinese tomato salad

ingredients

SERVES 4–6

2 large tomatoes

dressing

1 tbsp finely chopped
  scallions

1 tsp finely chopped garlic

$^1/_2$ tsp sesame oil

1 tbsp white rice vinegar

$^1/_2$ tsp salt

pinch of white pepper

pinch of sugar

method

1 Mix together all the ingredients for the dressing and set aside.

2 Thinly slice the tomatoes. Arrange on a plate and pour the dressing over the top. Serve immediately.

cabbage & cucumber in a vinegar dressing

ingredients

SERVES 4–6

8 oz/225 g Chinese cabbage, very finely shredded

1 tsp salt

1 cucumber, peeled, seeded, and finely chopped into short thin sticks

1 tsp sesame oil

2 tbsp white rice vinegar

1 tsp sugar

method

1 Sprinkle the cabbage with the salt and let stand for at least 10 minutes. Drain the cabbage if necessary, then mix with the cucumber pieces.

2 Whisk together the sesame oil, vinegar, and sugar and toss the vegetables in it. Serve immediately.

classic stir-fried vegetables

ingredients

SERVES 4

3 tbsp sesame oil

6 scallions, chopped finely,
   plus 2 scallions, chopped
   finely, to garnish

1 garlic clove, crushed

1 tbsp grated fresh gingerroot

1 head of broccoli,
   cut into florets

1 orange or yellow bell
   pepper, chopped coarsely

$4^1/_2$ oz/125 g red cabbage,
   shredded

$4^1/_2$ oz/125 g baby corn

6 oz/175 g portobello or large
   cup mushrooms, sliced
   thinly

7 oz/200 g/$1^1/_3$ cups fresh
   bean sprouts

9 oz/250 g canned water
   chestnuts, drained

4 tsp soy sauce, or to taste

cooked wild rice, to serve

method

1 Heat 2 tablespoons of the oil in a large skillet or wok over high heat. Stir-fry the 6 chopped scallions with the garlic and gingerroot for 30 seconds.

2 Add the broccoli, bell pepper, and red cabbage and stir-fry for 1–2 minutes. Mix in the baby corn and mushrooms and stir-fry for an additional 1–2 minutes.

3 Finally, add the bean sprouts and water chestnuts and cook for 2 minutes. Pour in the soy sauce and stir well.

4 Serve immediately over cooked wild rice, garnished with the remaining scallions.

sweet-&-sour vegetables with cashew nuts

ingredients

SERVES 4

1 tbsp vegetable or peanut oil

1 tsp chili oil

2 onions, sliced

2 carrots, thinly sliced

2 zucchini, thinly sliced

4 oz/115 g head of broccoli, cut into florets

4 oz/115 g white mushrooms, sliced

4 oz/115 g small bok choy, halved

2 tbsp jaggery or brown sugar

2 tbsp Thai soy sauce

1 tbsp rice vinegar

2 oz/55 g/scant $^1/_2$ cup cashew nuts

method

1 Heat both the oils in a preheated wok or skillet, add the onions, and stir-fry for 1–2 minutes until beginning to soften.

2 Add the carrots, zucchini, and broccoli and stir-fry for 2–3 minutes. Add the mushrooms, bok choy, sugar, soy sauce, and vinegar and stir-fry for 1–2 minutes.

3 Meanwhile, heat a dry, heavy-bottom skillet over high heat, add the cashew nuts, and cook, shaking the skillet frequently, until lightly toasted. Sprinkle the cashew nuts over the stir-fry and serve immediately.

vegetable & coconut curry

ingredients

SERVES 4

1 onion, coarsely chopped

3 garlic cloves, thinly sliced

1-inch/2.5-cm piece fresh
  gingerroot, thinly sliced

2 fresh green chiles, seeded
  and finely chopped

1 tbsp vegetable oil

1 tsp ground turmeric

1 tsp ground coriander

1 tsp ground cumin

2 lb 4 oz/1 kg mixed
  vegetables, such as
  cauliflower, zucchini,
  potatoes, carrots, and
  green beans, cut into
  chunks

7 oz/200 g/scant 1 cup
  coconut cream or milk

salt and pepper

2 tbsp chopped fresh cilantro,
  to garnish

freshly cooked rice, to serve

method

1 Put the onion, garlic, gingerroot, and chiles in a food processor and process until almost smooth.

2 Heat the oil in a large, heavy-bottom pan over medium-low heat, add the onion mixture, and cook, stirring constantly, for 5 minutes.

3 Add the turmeric, ground coriander, and cumin and cook, stirring frequently, for 3–4 minutes. Add the vegetables and stir to coat in the spice paste.

4 Add the coconut cream or milk to the vegetables, cover, and let simmer for 30–40 minutes until the vegetables are tender.

5 Season with salt and pepper, garnish with the chopped fresh cilantro, and serve with rice.

stir-fried green beans with red bell pepper

ingredients

SERVES 4–6

10 oz/280 g green beans, cut
   into 2$\frac{1}{2}$-inch/6-cm lengths
1 tbsp vegetable or peanut oil
1 red bell pepper, slivered
pinch of salt
pinch of sugar

method

1 Blanch the beans in a large pan of boiling water for 30 seconds. Drain and set aside.

2 In a preheated wok or deep pan, heat the oil and stir-fry the beans for 1 minute over high heat. Add the pepper and stir-fry for an additional 1 minute. Sprinkle the salt and sugar on top and serve.

spicy green beans

ingredients

SERVES 4

7 oz/200 g/generous 1^1/$_4$
   cups green beans,
   trimmed and cut
   diagonally into 3–4 pieces
2 tbsp vegetable or peanut oil
4 dried chiles, cut into
   2 or 3 pieces
^{1}/$_2$ tsp Szechuan peppers
1 garlic clove, finely sliced
6 thin slices of fresh
   gingerroot
2 scallions, white part only,
   cut diagonally into thin
   pieces
pinch of sea salt

method

1 Blanch the beans in a large pan of boiling water for 30 seconds. Drain and set aside.

2 In a preheated wok or deep pan, heat 1 tablespoon of the oil. Over low heat, stir-fry the beans for about 5 minutes, or until they are beginning to wrinkle. Remove from the wok and set aside.

3 Add the remaining oil and stir-fry the chiles and peppers until they are fragrant. Add the garlic, gingerroot, and scallions and stir-fry until they begin to soften. Throw in the beans and toss, then add the sea salt and serve immediately.

stir-fried broccoli

ingredients

SERVES 4

2 tbsp vegetable oil

2 medium heads of broccoli, cut into florets

2 tbsp soy sauce

1 tsp cornstarch

1 tbsp superfine sugar

1 tsp grated fresh gingerroot

1 garlic clove, crushed

pinch of hot chile flakes

1 tsp toasted sesame seeds, to garnish

method

1 In a large skillet or wok, heat the oil until almost smoking. Stir-fry the broccoli for 4–5 minutes.

2 In a small bowl, combine the soy sauce, cornstarch, sugar, gingerroot, garlic, and hot chile flakes. Add the mixture to the broccoli. Cook over gentle heat, stirring constantly, for 2–3 minutes until the sauce thickens slightly.

3 Transfer to a serving dish, garnish with the sesame seeds and serve immediately.

broccoli & snow pea stir-fry

ingredients

SERVES 4

2 tbsp vegetable or peanut oil

dash of sesame oil

1 garlic clove, finely chopped

8 oz/225 g head of broccoli,
  cut into small florets

4 oz/115 g/1 cup snow peas,
  trimmed

8 oz/225 g Chinese cabbage,
  chopped into $1/2$-inch/
  1-cm slices

5–6 scallions, finely chopped

$1/2$ tsp salt

2 tbsp light soy sauce

1 tbsp Shaoxing rice wine

1 tsp sesame seeds, lightly
  toasted

method

1 In a preheated wok or deep pan, heat the oils, then add the garlic and stir-fry vigorously. Add all the vegetables and salt and stir-fry over high heat, tossing rapidly, for about 3 minutes.

2 Pour in the light soy sauce and Shaoxing and cook for an additional 2 minutes. Sprinkle with the sesame seeds and serve hot.

choi sum in oyster sauce

ingredients

SERVES 4–6

10^1/$_2$ oz/300 g choi sum

1 tbsp vegetable or peanut oil

1 tsp finely chopped garlic

1 tbsp oyster sauce

method

1 Blanch the choi sum in a large pan of boiling water for 30 seconds. Drain and set aside.

2 In a preheated wok or deep pan, heat the oil and stir-fry the garlic until fragrant. Add the choi sum and toss for 1 minute. Stir in the oyster sauce and serve.

stir-fried chinese greens

ingredients

SERVES 4

1 tbsp vegetable or peanut oil

1 tsp finely chopped garlic

8 oz/225 g leafy Chinese
    greens, coarsely chopped

$^1/_2$ tsp salt

method

1 In a preheated wok or deep pan, heat the oil and stir-fry the garlic until fragrant.

2 Over high heat, toss in the Chinese greens and salt and stir-fry for 1 minute maximum. Serve immediately.

hot-&-sour cabbage

ingredients

SERVES 4

1 lb/450 g firm white cabbage

1 tbsp vegetable or peanut oil

10 Szechuan peppers or
more, to taste

3 dried chiles, coarsely
chopped

$1/2$ tsp salt

1 tsp white rice vinegar

dash of sesame oil

pinch of sugar

method

1 To prepare the cabbage, discard the outer leaves and tough stems. Chop the cabbage into $1^1/_4$-inch/3-cm squares, breaking up the chunks. Rinse thoroughly in cold water.

2 In a preheated wok or deep pan, heat the oil and cook the peppers until fragrant. Stir in the chiles. Throw in the cabbage, a little at a time, together with the salt, and stir-fry for 2 minutes.

3 Add the vinegar, sesame oil, and sugar and cook for an additional minute, or until the cabbage is tender. Serve immediately.

garlic spinach stir-fry

ingredients

SERVES 4

6 tbsp vegetable oil

6 garlic cloves, crushed

2 tbsp black bean sauce

3 tomatoes, coarsely chopped

2 lb/900 g spinach, tough
stalks removed, coarsely
chopped

1 tsp chili sauce, or to taste

2 tbsp fresh lemon juice

salt and pepper

method

1 Heat the oil in a preheated wok or large skillet over high heat, add the garlic, black bean sauce, and tomatoes and stir-fry for 1 minute.

2 Stir in the spinach, chili sauce, and lemon juice and mix well. Cook, stirring frequently, for 3 minutes, or until the spinach is just wilted. Season with salt and pepper. Remove from the heat and serve immediately.

chunky potatoes with cilantro leaves

ingredients

SERVES 6–8

4 potatoes, peeled and cut
into large chunks

vegetable or peanut oil,
for frying

3^1/$_2$ oz/100 g/scant 1 cup
pork, not too lean, finely
chopped or ground

1 green bell pepper, finely
chopped

1 tbsp finely chopped
scallions, white part only

2 tsp salt

^{1}/$_2$ tsp white pepper

pinch of sugar

2–3 tbsp cooking water from
the potatoes

2 tbsp chopped cilantro
leaves

method

1 Boil the potatoes in a large pan of boiling water for 15–25 minutes, or until cooked. Drain, reserving some of the water.

2 In a wok or deep pan, heat plenty of the oil and cook the potatoes until golden. Drain and set aside.

3 In the clean preheated wok or pan, heat 1 tablespoon of the oil and stir-fry the pork, bell pepper, and scallions for 1 minute. Season with the salt, pepper, and sugar and stir-fry for an additional 1 minute.

4 Stir in the potato chunks and add the water. Cook for 2–3 minutes, or until the potatoes are warmed through. Turn off the heat, then stir in the cilantro and serve warm.

szechuan fried eggplant

ingredients

SERVES 4

vegetable or peanut oil,
for frying

4 eggplants, halved
lengthwise and cut
diagonally into 2-inch/
5-cm pieces

1 tbsp chili bean sauce

2 tsp finely chopped fresh
gingerroot

2 tsp finely chopped garlic

2–3 tbsp chicken stock

1 tsp sugar

1 tsp light soy sauce

3 scallions, finely chopped

method

1 In a preheated wok or deep pan, heat the oil and cook the eggplant pieces for 3–4 minutes, or until lightly browned. Drain on paper towels and set aside.

2 In the clean wok or deep pan, heat 2 tablespoons of the oil. Add the chili bean sauce and stir-fry rapidly, then add the gingerroot and garlic and stir until fragrant. Add the stock, sugar, and light soy sauce. Toss in the fried eggplant pieces and let simmer for 2 minutes. Stir in the scallions and serve.

eggplant with red bell peppers

ingredients

SERVES 4

3 tbsp vegetable or peanut oil

1 garlic clove, finely chopped

3 eggplants, halved
  lengthwise and cut
  diagonally into 1-inch/
  2.5-cm pieces

1 tsp white rice vinegar

1 red bell pepper, finely sliced

2 tbsp light soy sauce

1 tsp sugar

1 tbsp finely chopped cilantro
  leaves, to garnish

method

1 In a preheated wok or deep pan, heat the oil. When it begins to smoke, toss in the garlic and stir-fry until fragrant, then add the eggplant. Stir-fry for 30 seconds, then add the vinegar. Turn down the heat and cook, covered, for 5 minutes, stirring occasionally.

2 When the eggplant pieces are soft, add the bell pepper and stir. Add the light soy sauce and sugar and cook, uncovered, for 2 minutes.

3 Turn off the heat and rest for 2 minutes. Transfer to a dish, then garnish with cilantro and serve.

oyster mushrooms & vegetables with peanut chili sauce

ingredients

SERVES 4

1 tbsp sesame oil

4 scallions, sliced finely

1 carrot, cut into batons

1 zucchini, cut into batons

1/2 head of broccoli,
    cut into florets

1 lb/450 g oyster mushrooms,
    sliced thinly

2 tbsp coarse peanut butter

1 tsp chili powder, or to taste

3 tbsp water

cooked rice or noodles,
    to serve

wedges of lime, to garnish

method

1 Heat the oil in a skillet or wok until almost smoking. Stir-fry the scallions for 1 minute. Add the carrot and zucchini and stir-fry for an additional 1 minute. Then add the broccoli and cook for 1 minute more.

2 Stir in the mushrooms and cook until they are soft and at least half the liquid they produce has evaporated. Add the peanut butter and stir well. Season with the chili powder. Finally, add the water and cook for an additional 1 minute.

3 Serve over rice or noodles and garnish with wedges of lime.

braised straw mushrooms

ingredients

SERVES 4

1 tbsp vegetable or peanut oil

1 tsp finely chopped garlic

6 oz/175 g straw mushrooms,
washed but left whole

2 tsp fermented black beans,
rinsed and lightly mashed

1 tsp sugar

1 tbsp light soy sauce

1 tsp dark soy sauce

method

1 Heat the oil in a small claypot or pan. Cook the garlic until fragrant, then add the mushrooms and stir well to coat in the oil.

2 Add the beans, sugar, and soy sauces, then lower the heat and let simmer, covered, for about 10 minutes, or until the mushrooms are soft.

bamboo shoots with bean curd

ingredients

SERVES 4–6

3 dried Chinese mushrooms,
　soaked in warm water for
　20 minutes

2 oz/55 g baby bok choy

vegetable or peanut oil, for
　deep-frying

1 lb/450 g firm bean curd,
　cut into 1-inch/2.5-cm
　squares

2 oz/55 g/$^1\!/_2$ cup fresh or
　canned bamboo shoots,
　rinsed and finely sliced (if
　using fresh shoots, boil in
　water first for 30 minutes)

1 tsp oyster sauce

1 tsp light soy sauce

method

1 Squeeze out any excess water from the mushrooms and finely slice, discarding any tough stems. Blanch the bok choy in a large pan of boiling water for 30 seconds. Drain and set aside.

2 Heat enough oil for deep-frying in a wok, deep-fat fryer, or large heavy-bottom pan until it reaches 350–375°F/180–190°C, or until a cube of bread browns in 30 seconds. Cook the bean curd cubes until golden brown. Remove, then drain and set aside.

3 In a preheated wok or deep pan, heat 1 tablespoon of the oil, then toss in the mushrooms and bok choy and stir. Add the bean curd and bamboo shoots with the oyster and soy sauces. Heat through and serve.

stir-fried bean sprouts

ingredients

SERVES 4

1 tbsp vegetable or peanut oil

8 oz/225 g/generous $1^1/_2$
    cups bean sprouts,
    trimmed

2 tbsp finely chopped
    scallions

$^1/_2$ tsp salt

pinch of sugar

method

1 In a preheated wok or deep pan, heat the oil and stir-fry the bean sprouts with the scallions for about 1 minute. Add the salt and sugar and stir.

2 Remove from the heat and serve immediately.

egg-fried rice

ingredients

SERVES 4

2 tbsp vegetable or peanut oil

12 oz/350 g cooked rice, chilled

1 egg, well beaten

method

1 Heat the oil in a preheated wok or deep pan and stir-fry the rice for 1 minute, breaking it down as much as possible into individual grains.

2 Quickly add the egg, stirring, so as to coat each piece of rice. Stir until the egg is cooked and the rice, as far as possible, is in single grains. Serve immediately.

steamed white rice

ingredients

SERVES 3–4

8 oz/225 g/generous 1 cup
   rice

cold water

method

1 Wash the rice. Place in a pan with the same volume of water plus a little extra (the water should just cover the rice). Bring to a boil, then cover and let simmer for about 15 minutes.

2 Turn off the heat and let the rice continue to cook in its own steam for about 5 minutes. At this point, the grains should be cooked through but not sticking together.

desserts

If the highlight of your visit to your favorite Chinese restaurant is the moment when the waiter sets down a plate of Banana Fritters or Toffee Apple Slices in front of you, then this chapter will really appeal to you!

In authentic Chinese cuisine, the sweet things that are known as "desserts" in the Western world are either eaten separately from a meal, or are served as part of the meal whenever they happen to be ready. They are also eaten as snacks at any time of the day. Baked sweet treats, such as Almond Cookies, have only recently been added to the repertoire, there being no oven in a traditional Chinese kitchen. Seasonal fruit, perhaps with a little sugar added, is the most popular dessert in China—Fresh Fruit Salad with Lemon Juice is a simple but refreshing dish, and looks very attractive made with different varieties of melon. For a more sophisticated fruit-based recipe, Mango Pudding blends East with West with great success.

Chinese rice puddings are made with glutinous rice, which is soaked in cold water for at least 2 hours before it is cooked. For an impressive end to a festive Chinese meal, Eight-treasures Sweet Rice Cake, layered with dried fruits and sweet red bean paste, will please your palate and also bring you luck!

pears in honey syrup

ingredients

SERVES 4

4 medium-ripe pears

7 fl oz/200 ml/generous
   ³/₄ cup water

1 tsp sugar

1 tbsp honey

method

1 Peel each pear, leaving the stem intact. Wrap each one in aluminum foil and place in a pan with the stems resting on the side of the pan. Add enough water to cover at least half of the height of the pears. Bring to a boil and let simmer for 30 minutes. Remove the pears and carefully remove the foil, reserving any juices. Set the pears aside to cool.

2 Bring the measured water to a boil. Add any pear juices, the sugar, and the honey and boil for 5 minutes. Remove from the heat and let cool a little.

3 To serve, place each pear in a small individual dish. Pour over a little syrup and serve just warm.

fresh fruit salad with lemon juice

ingredients

SERVES 4–6

2 tbsp sugar

1 lb/450 g mixed melons,
    cut into balls or cubes

2 bananas, thinly sliced
    diagonally

juice of 1 lemon

method

1 In a large bowl, sprinkle the sugar over the melon pieces.

2 Toss the banana in the lemon juice and add to the melon, then serve immediately.

mango pudding

ingredients

SERVES 6

1 oz/25 g sago, soaked in water
   for at least 20 minutes
8 fl oz/250 ml/1 cup warm
   water
2 tablespoons sugar
1 large ripe mango, weighing
   about 10 oz/280 g
7 fl oz/200 ml/generous
   $^3/_4$ cup whipping cream
1 tbsp powdered gelatin,
   dissolved in 8 fl oz/250 ml/
   1 cup warm water

method

1 Put the drained sago and warm water in a pan. Bring to a boil and then cook over low heat for 10 minutes, stirring frequently, until thick. Stir in the sugar and let cool.

2 Peel the mango and slice off the flesh from the pit. Reduce the mango to a smooth paste in a food processor or blender. Stir in the cream and then the gelatin.

3 Combine all the ingredients. Pour into 6 small bowls and let chill in the refrigerator until set.

toffee bananas

ingredients

SERVES 4

$2^1/2$ oz/70 g/$^1/2$ cup self-rising
    flour

1 egg, beaten

5 tbsp iced water

4 large, ripe bananas

3 tbsp lemon juice

2 tbsp rice flour

vegetable oil, for deep-frying

caramel

4 oz/115 g/generous $^1/2$ cup
    superfine sugar

4 tbsp iced water, plus an
    extra bowl of iced water
    for setting

2 tbsp sesame seeds

method

1 Sift the flour into a bowl. Make a well in the center, add the egg and 5 tablespoons of the iced water and beat from the center outward, until combined into a smooth batter.

2 Peel the bananas and cut into 2-inch/5-cm pieces. Gently shape them into balls with your hands. Brush with lemon juice to prevent discoloration, then roll them in rice flour until coated.

3 Pour oil into a pan to a depth of $2^1/2$ inches/ 6 cm and preheat to 350–375°F/180–190°C, or until a cube of bread browns in 30 seconds. Coat the balls in the batter and cook in batches in the hot oil for about 2 minutes each, until golden. Lift them out and drain on paper towels.

4 To make the caramel, put the sugar into a small pan over low heat. Add 4 tablespoons of iced water and heat, stirring, until the sugar dissolves. Let simmer for 5 minutes, remove from the heat, and stir in the sesame seeds. Toss the banana balls in the caramel, scoop them out, and drop into the bowl of iced water to set. Lift them out and divide among individual serving bowls. Serve hot.

banana fritters

ingredients

SERVES 4

2½ oz/70 g/½ cup
   all-purpose flour
2 tbsp rice flour
1 tbsp superfine sugar
1 egg, separated
5 fl oz/150 ml/⅔ cup
   coconut milk
4 large bananas
sunflower oil for deep-frying

1 tsp confectioners' sugar,
   1 tsp ground cinnamon
   and lime wedges, to
   decorate

method

1 Sift the all-purpose flour, rice flour, and sugar into a bowl and make a well in the center. Add the egg yolk and coconut milk. Beat the mixture until a smooth, thick batter forms.

2 Whisk the egg white in a clean, dry bowl until stiff enough to hold soft peaks. Fold it into the batter lightly and evenly.

3 Heat a 2½-inch/6-cm depth of oil in a large pan to 350–375°F/180–190°C, or until a cube of bread browns in 30 seconds. Cut the bananas in half crosswise, then dip them quickly into the batter to coat them.

4 Drop the bananas carefully into the hot oil and deep-fry in batches for 2–3 minutes until golden brown, turning once.

5 Drain on paper towels. Sprinkle with confectioners' sugar and cinnamon and serve immediately, with lime wedges for squeezing juice as desired.

toffee apple slices

ingredients

SERVES 4

4 apples, peeled, cored, and
    each cut into thick slices
vegetable or peanut oil, for
    deep-frying

batter

4 oz/115 g/^{2}/$_3$ cup
    all-purpose flour
1 egg, beaten
4 fl oz/125 ml/^{1}/$_2$ cup
    cold water

toffee syrup

4 tbsp sesame oil
8 oz/225 g/scant 1^1/$_4$ cups
    sugar
2 tbsp sesame seeds, toasted

method

1 To prepare the batter, sift the flour and stir in the egg. Slowly add the water, beating to form a smooth and thick batter. Dip each apple slice in the batter.

2 Heat enough oil for deep-frying in a wok, deep-fat fryer, or large heavy-bottom pan until it reaches 350–375°F/180–190°C, or until a cube of bread browns in 30 seconds. Deep-fry the apple slices until golden brown. Drain and set aside.

3 To make the toffee syrup, heat the sesame oil in a small, heavy-bottom pan and, when beginning to smoke, add the sugar, stirring constantly, until the mixture caramelizes and turns golden. Remove from the heat, then stir in the sesame seeds and pour into a large flat pan.

4 Over very low heat, place the apple slices in the syrup, turning once. When coated, dip each slice in cold water. Serve immediately.

almond jelly in ginger sauce

ingredients

SERVES 6–8

jelly

30 fl oz/940 ml/3³/₄ cups
   water

¹/₈ oz/5 g agar-agar

8 oz/225 g/scant 1¹/₄ cups
   sugar

4 fl oz/125 ml/¹/₂ cup
   evaporated milk

1 tsp almond extract

sauce

3¹/₂ oz/100 g piece of fresh
   gingerroot, coarsely
   chopped

30 fl oz/940 ml/3³/₄ cups
   water

2 oz/55 g/generous ¹/₄ cup
   brown sugar

method

1 To prepare the jelly, bring the water to a boil. Add the agar-agar and stir until dissolved. Stir in the sugar.

2 Pour through a strainer into a shallow dish. Pour in the evaporated milk, stirring constantly. When slightly cooled, stir in the almond extract, then let chill in the refrigerator.

3 To make the ginger sauce, boil the gingerroot, water, and sugar in a covered pan for at least 1¹/₂ hours, or until the sauce is golden in color. Discard the gingerroot.

4 With a knife, cut thin slices of the jelly and arrange in individual bowls. Pour a little ginger sauce, warm or cold, over the jelly.

eight-treasures sweet rice cake

ingredients

SERVES 6–8

8 oz/225 g/generous 1 cup glutinous rice, soaked in cold water for at least 2 hours

3^1/2 oz/100 g/^{1}/2 cup sugar

2 tablespoons shortening

2 dried kumquats, finely chopped

3 prunes, finely chopped

5 dried red dates, soaked for 20 minutes in warm water, then finely chopped

1 tsp raisins

12 lotus seeds (if using dried seeds, soak in warm water for at least 1 hour)

3^1/2 oz/100 g sweet red bean paste

method

1 Steam the glutinous rice for about 20 minutes, or until soft. Set aside. When the rice is cool, mix in the sugar and shortening by hand to form a sticky mass.

2 Arrange the dried fruits and seeds in the base of a clear pudding basin. Top with half the rice mixture, then press down tightly and smooth the top.

3 Spread the bean paste on top of the rice, and top with the remaining rice mixture. Press down and smooth the top.

4 Steam for 20 minutes and cool slightly, then turn out onto a plate. Cut into small slices at the table.

winter rice pudding with dried fruits

ingredients

SERVES 6–8

1 tbsp peanuts

1 tbsp pine nuts

1 tbsp lotus seeds

8 oz/225 g mixed dried fruits
   (raisins, kumquats,
   prunes, dates, etc.)

64 fl oz/2 liters/8 cups water

4 oz/115 g/generous $1/2$ cup
   sugar

8 oz/225 g/generous 1 cup
   glutinous rice, soaked in
   cold water for at least
   2 hours

method

1 Soak the peanuts, pine nuts, and lotus seeds in a bowl of cold water for at least 1 hour. Soak the dried fruits as necessary. Chop all larger fruits into small pieces.

2 Bring the water to a boil in a pan, then add the sugar and stir until dissolved. Add the drained rice, nuts, lotus seeds, and mixed dried fruits. Bring back to a boil. Cover and let simmer over very low heat for 1 hour, stirring frequently.

almond cookies

ingredients

MAKES ABOUT 50

1 lb 8 oz/675 g/4$^{1}/_{2}$ cups
    all-purpose flour
$^{1}/_{2}$ tsp baking powder
$^{1}/_{2}$ tsp salt
3$^{1}/_{2}$ oz/100 g slivered almonds
8 oz/225 g shortening, cut
    into tiny cubes
8 oz/225 g/generous 1 cup
    white sugar
1 egg, lightly beaten
1$^{1}/_{2}$ tsp almond extract
50 whole almonds,
    to decorate (optional)

method

1 Sift the flour, baking powder, and salt together and set aside.

2 Pulverize the almond slivers in a food processor, then add the flour mixture and pulse until the nuts are well mixed with the flour.

3 Turn the flour and nut mixture into a large bowl, then add the shortening and work into the flour until crumbly. Add the sugar, egg, and almond extract and mix well until the dough is soft and pliable but still firm enough to be handled.

4 Divide the dough into small 1-inch/2.5-cm balls. Place the balls 2 inches/5 cm apart on an ungreased cookie sheet and flatten them into circles with the back of a spoon. Press a whole almond into the center of each, if liked.

5 Preheat the oven to 325°F/160°C and bake the cookies for 15–18 minutes, or until just beginning to brown, then remove and turn out onto a cooling rack.

a
almond
almond cookies 238
almond jelly in ginger
sauce 232
ants climbing a tree 122

b
baby squid stuffed with
pork & mushrooms 112
bamboo shoots with bean
curd 210
banana fritters 228
bang bang chicken 78
bean curd & bean sprout
soup 14
beef
beef chop suey 56
beef noodles with
oyster sauce 118
braised straw mushrooms
208
broccoli & snow pea
stir-fry 190

c
cabbage & cucumber in a
vinegar dressing 176
chicken
chicken & green
vegetables 140
chicken chow mein 142
chicken chow mein
baskets 144
chicken fried rice 136
chicken-sesame salad
146
chicken with cashew
nuts 80
chiles stuffed with fish
paste 90
choi sum in oyster sauce
192
chunky potatoes with
cilantro leaves 200
clams in black bean
sauce 104
classic stir-fried
vegetables 178
congee with fish fillet 150
crab
crab & corn soup 10
crab fried rice 154
crispy dishes
crab wontons 40
duck 84
cross the bridge noodles
148

d
deep-fried river fish with
chili bean sauce 98
dumplings in a cold spicy
sauce 32

e
egg
egg-fried rice 214
egg-fried rice with peas
166
egg fu yung 158
eggplant with red bell
peppers 204
eight-treasures sweet rice
cake 234

f
firepot of mushrooms &
bean curd 170
five-willow fish 94
fresh fruit salad with
lemon juice 222
fried dishes
fish with pine nuts 88
rice with pork & shrimp
132

g
garlic spinach stir-fry 198
ginger
ginger beef with yellow
bell peppers 62
ginger chicken with
toasted sesame
seeds 82
ginger shrimp with
oyster mushrooms
106
gong bao chicken 76
ground beef & cilantro
soup 12

h
hoisin pork with garlic
noodles 130
hot sesame beef 58
hot-&-sour dishes
cabbage 196
noodle salad 162
soup 16

l
lettuce wraps 44

m
mango pudding 224

marinated beef with
vegetables 54
mushroom soup 20

o
onion pancakes 46
oyster mushrooms &
vegetables with peanut
chili sauce 206

p
pears in honey syrup 220
Peking dishes
duck 86
duck salad 134
pickled baby cucumbers
42
pork
pork & ginger
dumplings 28
pork lo mein 124

r
rice sticks with beef in
black bean sauce 120

s
seafood chow mein 152
shrimp
salad 156
shrimp, snow peas &
cashew nuts 108
shrimp toasts 38
simple stir-fried scallops
100
Singapore noodles 126
soft-wrapped pork &
shrimp rolls 26
sour-&-spicy pork 128
soy chicken wings 34
spareribs in a sweet-&-
sour sauce 72
spicy dishes
bean curd 168
green beans 186
Szechuan pork 68
spring rolls 30
steamed dishes
sole with black bean
sauce 96
white rice 216
stir-fried dishes
bean sprouts 212
beef with broccoli &
ginger 60

broccoli 188
Chinese greens 194

fresh crab with ginger
110
green beans with red
bell pepper 184
scallops with asparagus
102
sweet chile squid 114
sweet-&-sour dishes
chicken 74
noodles with chicken
138
vegetables on noodle
pancakes 164
vegetables with cashew
nuts 180
Szechuan dishes
fried eggplant 202
noodles 160
pork & bell pepper 70
pumpkin soup 24

t
tea-scented eggs 50
toffee
toffee apple slices 230
toffee bananas 226
tomato salad 174

v
vegetables
vegetable & coconut
curry 182
vegetable soup 22
vegetarian spring rolls
48

w
whitebait with green chili
36
whole chicken soup 18
whole deep-fried fish with
soy & ginger 92
winter rice pudding with
dried fruits 236
wonton soup 8

x
Xinjiang dishes
lamb casserole 66
rice pot with lamb 64